FIT IN, STAND OUT

FIT IN, STAND OUT

Mastering the FISO Factor
for Success in Business and Life

Blythe J. McGarvie

McGraw-Hill

New York Chicago San Francisco Lisbon London
Madrid Mexico City Milan New Delhi San Juan Seoul
Singapore Sydney Toronto

1 2 3 4 5 6 7 8 9 0 DOC/DOC 0 9 8 7 6 5

ISBN 0-07-146079-9

McGraw-Hill books are available at special discounts to use as premiums and sales promotions, or for use in corporate training programs. For more information, please write to the Director of Special Sales, Professional Publishing, McGraw-Hill, Two Penn Plaza, New York, NY 10121-2298. Or contact your local bookstore.

 This book is printed on recycled, acid-free paper containing a minimum of 50% recycled de-inked paper.

Library of Congress Cataloging-in-Publication Data
McGarvie, Blythe J.
  Fit it, stand out : mastering the FISO factor for success in business & life / by Blythe J. McGarvie.
      p. cm.
  Includes bibliographical references and index.
  ISBN 0-07-146079-9 (alk. paper)
  1. Executive ability.   2. Leadership.   3. Interpersonal relations.   4. Performance.   5. Success in business.   I. Title.
  HD38.2.M3937 2006
  650.1'3—dc22
                                                                    2005016462

CONTENTS

Foreword   ix
Author's Note   xiii
Introduction   xvii

Chapter 1: The Everyday Work of Leaders   1
    Ambitious but Unprepared   3
    Often Forgotten Precepts   7
    Leaders Are Systems Thinkers   9
    The Two Imperatives of a Dynamic Business System   11

Chapter 2: Fit In and Stand Out   17
    Navigating Through the Corporate Wonderland   18
    Fitting-In   20
    Standing-Out   25
    The FISO Factor   29

Chapter 3: The Catalytic Agents of the FISO Factor   33
 The FISO Factor Catalysts   35
  Financial Acuity   35
  Integrity   39
  Linkages   42
  Learning   44
  Perspective   46
  Global Citizenship   47
 The FISO Factor Catalysts and Your
 Leadership Platform   49

Chapter 4: Financial Acuity: The Language of Business   53
 Cracking the Corporate Code   55
  Learn the Basics   57
  Identify Your Financial Focus   59
  Frame Your Work   61
 The Habits of Financially Acute Leaders   64
  Dig into the Numbers   64
  Act on Your Findings   65
  Foster Financial Acuity Companywide   66
 Financial Acuity Yields Confidence   68

Chapter 5: Integrity: The Leader's North Star   71
 Beyond Legal Compliance   74
  Ethics   75
  Soundness   76
  Completeness   78
 The Demands of Integrity   80
 Organizational Integrity   83
 Integrity Yields Trust   86

Chapter 6: Linkages: The Lever of Alliance   89
 The Competitive Advantage of Linkages   92
  Opportunity   92
  Creativity   93
  Productivity   95

Creating and Maintaining Linkages   96
   Create a Robust Network of Linkages   97
   Focus on Giving Instead of Getting   100
   Practice the "Touch-Tone Approach" to
     Linkages   101
The Linked Organization   103
Linkages Yield Access   107

Chapter 7: Learning: The Wellspring of Renewal   109
   Adopt and Adapt   112
     Adopt   112
       Tap the Sources of Learning   113
       Ask Astute Questions   115
       Listen!   116
     Adapt   119
       Reflect   119
       Connect   120
   Apply Learning with the Five A's   121
     Perfection Is the Enemy of Progress   123
     Past Performance Can Provide Future
       Knowledge   124
     Failure Is Inevitable, but Large Losses
       Are Not   124
   Create a Learning Organization   126
   Learning Yields Innovation   128

Chapter 8: Perspective: The Prism of Insight   131
   The Leader's Perspective   134
   Gaining Other People's Perspectives   137
     Empathize to Identify Perspective   137
     Become a Perspective Magnet   140
     Utilize Perspective to Build Consensus   143
   Creating Organizational Perspective   145
   Perspective Yields Balanced Judgment   150

Chapter 9: Global Citizenship: The Passport
  to Opportunity 153
    Getting Prepared for Global Leadership 156
      Transcend Nationality 156
      Learn from the World 160
      *Stimulate Global Coordination
        and Cooperation 162*
    Building the Global Organization 165
      Global Strategies 165
      Global Knowledge 166
      Global Management 167
    Global Citizenship Yields Agility 169

Epilogue: Choosing Your Path 173
    Fit In or Stand Out? 174
      Corporate Culture 174
      Position in Company 177
    Navigating the Journey 178
      *Can I Contribute to the Success
        of the Company? 181*
      Will I Learn Something from This? 181
      *Is the Company Ready to Do What
        Needs to Be Done? 183*
    The Final Word on Success 184

Notes 185
Acknowledgments 201
Index 203

FOREWORD

The time is right for this book. Already, in the first few years of this century, there have been an extraordinary number of events and circumstances that have changed how we do business. We know that globalization and technology have leveled the playing field, putting Boston, Beijing, and Bangalore on nearly equal footing. We know that talent has no borders. We know that competition lurks where one hasn't begun to look. We know that corporations exist in an ever-connected global community and are, themselves, expected to act as responsible citizens.

It is no wonder that the stakes are higher for businesses today—and for the people who run them. So stop for a moment and consider: Who will choose to step up and lead our enterprises of the future? Presumably it's only going to get tougher.

In this context, Blythe McGarvie has written a practical book for the aspiring leader. I applaud her for recognizing this need. I sense an urgency among senior executives to develop the next generation of leaders. With this book, Blythe makes an important contribution. She guides the aspiring leader on a journey to resolve the inherent contradiction between fitting in and standing out. Master this balance, and the highest levels of performance are within reach.

I have known Blythe for several years. Both as an author and businesswoman, Blythe uniquely blends deep analytical skills and financial acumen with a real passion and charisma for the power of effective leadership. And while her writing is grounded in theory, her words are pragmatic, compelling, and clear.

Blythe lives the principles she describes. She is a student of her theories about relationships, and her own inquisitiveness and continuous learning enable her to connect many dots. Throughout the book, she draws upon examples of leaders who have reached the summit of their professions, as well as her own experiences on the path to effective leadership. This book will be devoured by those aspiring to make the trip.

The paradox of fitting in yet standing out—the yin and yang of leadership as she calls it—mirrors my own experience. Very early in my career, when I held positions that didn't have much authority, I learned the hard way to build linkages and relationships that I could call upon to influence an outcome. I wish I'd had this book.

Fitting in is about those linkages. They are an essential element of effective organizations and effective leaders. They form the basis of high-performance teams whose members work across boundaries, willing to collaborate and freely share what they know.

Looked at another way, companies win not purely as a result of their strategies, clever ideas, or industry-leading operations. All are important, but winning ultimately comes down to attracting, developing, and retaining the best leaders on the planet—and creating roles for those people to fit in and succeed.

In fact, in my experience, a leader's job is to make it *attractive* to fit in. Most people are "volunteers" at work. They have options. So the leader must integrate a diverse range of experiences and capabilities on the team, as well as create an environment where motivated people have the desire and drive to do extraordinary things. At the end of the day, the leader has only the power of those people who have chosen to follow.

Blythe writes about six "catalytic agents" that support the imperatives of fitting in and standing out. I want to comment on three of them, which from my observations, can set great leaders apart from their peers:

I can't emphasize enough the importance of Blythe's chapter on integrity. She asks, how can you lead without moral authority? I have spent my entire career at Accenture, and we have had a set of core values embedded in our culture since day one. Among these is the value of integrity. I will venture so far as to say that the most important asset of a company today is the trust of its customers, employees, and stakeholders. This has never been more crucial. Leaders can't just talk about integrity. It needs to be part of them—a natural instinct seen in the leader's actions and interactions with individuals and groups.

I also appreciate Blythe's attention to financial acuity—an absolute requirement for being what I call "boardroom relevant." You must understand how your company makes money and how your customers make money. I'd also add execution to the mix. The best leaders know that the performance advantage of their organization versus their key competitors comes down to very minute differences. Execution, therefore, is paramount. And to execute well, you need to speak the language of business.

Lastly, I'll comment on Blythe's description of learning as the wellspring of renewal. The most successful leaders I have known have made learning a cornerstone of their personal development, as well as how they run their organizations. Blythe underscores this point. The reality is, leaders do not have all the answers to the many questions they face. And quite frankly, the ability to put ego aside and ask for help, engage different views, and challenge one's thinking is an absolute requirement for leadership success. I often tell my teams that if they find themselves operating in a very comfortable zone for more than a week, they are most likely not learning or growing. Getting those sweaty palms is a sure way to stay relevant—and have more fun.

One final note before you read the book: Over the course of the leadership journey, every leader experiences some very high points and some very low ones. The low points are what tends to separate the best leaders from the rest. The people who emerge from economic downturns and tough times are winners who make no excuses. They refuse to be seen as victims.

The leaders who rise to the top are approachable. They roll up their sleeves and fit into their teams. At the same time, they stand out as beacons of confidence and trust. They lead from the front as stewards of the organization, its brand, reputation, values, and people.

This is the portrait Blythe paints of the effective leader. Her book is a wealth of wisdom for the next generation who will choose to lead the future of business.

> Joe W. Forehand
> Chairman, Accenture
> June 30, 2005

AUTHOR'S NOTE

I knew when I was 14 that I wanted to be a CPA—not a CEO, but a CPA. To me, it was all about paying attention. I had a natural curiosity about what people did in their jobs. I saw how hard my folks worked for their three kids and to pay the mortgage. I remember my mom writing on the backs of envelopes, scribbling figures to make sure that the bills would be paid, mostly on time. She was an inner-city grammar school teacher in the Chicago Public Schools. She generally hated her job and told me never to become a teacher.

My dad taught at the college level as a professor of marketing and general business and liked it—but he had to do lots of other things, too. He shoveled coal in the apartment building in which we lived. He worked a couple of teaching jobs. He seemed always to be racing from one job to another, yet he squeezed in the time through at least eight years to study and work toward his PhD.

I started asking my parents' friends and neighbors about their jobs, if they actually *liked* their jobs. And if so, would they recommend their choice of career to their daughter or son. It was interesting that throughout this 14-year-old's unscientific survey, out of all the different jobs that came up, two were mentioned very consistently: doctor and CPA. In a lot of these people's lives the person's father had been a doctor or a CPA. Since I was good in math and liked it, the thought of being a certified public accountant seemed fun and rewarding and at least a little bit more secure than what we were accustomed to at home.

Funny then, how I wound up at a school that had neither an undergrad business nor an accounting program. I'd shot fairly high, only to be shot down by several Ivies, so I went to Northwestern, where I majored in economics. I decided during my junior year to apply to the graduate business school to study accounting in a special program that allowed me to start graduate studies during my senior year and skip a year of school. Sure enough, I found myself sitting for the grueling three-day CPA exam during my second year in business school. I figured if I passed the test on my first attempt, it meant I might have some talent in this direction. It also gave me confidence that I could succeed in the field—perhaps even to the level of chief financial officer at a major company. I wasn't aware of any women who were CFOs at the time, but I thought, well, there must be some out there *somewhere*. By 1994, I was one of ten female CFOs in the Fortune 500 and enjoying it.

After 25 years in the workforce, my chosen field not only semed secure but provided me the intellectual stimulation and opportunity to contribute that I had craved. Then, the Enron scandal hit the press. Next, Arthur Andersen & Co, my first fulltime employer, disappeared from the face of the earth. These events changed my world.

Being at just one company as a CFO no longer seemed like the only choice. I felt a need to help restore trust in business. I wanted to show how people can make money in business legally, maintaining independent integrity *and still have fun doing it.* I decided to leave my position to begin a consulting and speaking career to help others find 'the joy of business.'

Fortunately for me, I had built a bit of a reputation as a leading authority on leadership and change through my work and travel. A leading speakers' bureau based in Washington, DC, asked to represent me in my speaking career. Through it and the mining of network resources, I have been able to speak to many different organizations throughout this country and abroad and contribute to their further successes. What I have learned as a leader and innovator is now encapsulated here in this book.

Another dream I had—to be a board member— increasingly seemed to be compatible with my new career in public speaking. I'd observed that many of the public speakers I most admired and all of the real decision-makers in Chicago, a major base of mine, had served or were serving on corporate boards.

When the call came, to be interviewed for a board position at an east coast convenience store company called Wawa, I jumped at it. I didn't know how special the company was until I met with the chairman. So it was that my first company board experience began in 1998 at the age of 41 with Wawa, Inc., now the 70th largest privately-held company in the United States and probably the major innovator in its industry. When I first joined the board, seven years ago, the company had $1 billion in sales. Last year, we hit $3 billion. The company is quite profitable and expected to grow by 20 percent this year.

Since then, I have joined four public boards. I'm continually inspired and tested through my service on these major public boards, but these experiences have only reinforced the lessons learned earlier. I presently serve on the boards of: Accenture, the world's largest technology consulting and outsourcing company; Pepsi Bottling Group, a $11 billion consumer goods company with businesses throughout the world; St. Paul Travelers Companies, the leading property and casualty insurance company in the United States; and Lafarge North America, the largest diversified construction materials supplier on this continent.

Today all businesses exist in a global economy, and I bring extensive foreign experience to my understanding of business. I have traveled extensively around the world, including two weeks in Japan (under the auspices of the Chicago Council on Foreign Relations) to study the steel industry and to understand its markets. I have lived in France while a CFO for Société BIC, and I traveled widely in the Pacific Rim as the CAO for Sara Lee. During my time abroad, my French improved to the point that I felt comfortable presenting in French to the company's shareholders and analysts at annual meetings. The global perspective from these experiences has shaped the arguments and suggestions you will read here.

What does it all come down to? My passion now is to spread the word about taking charge of life and how this self-direction relates to business success. I like to quote Oscar Wilde, who said, "Life is not a dress rehearsal." I saw my parents persevere toward their goals. I figured that I should do the same. But, I have learned that perseverance is not enough. One must behave and perform so as to be part of a company, but also to be noticed—and not merely for being different. I've realized that the real challenge in a time of massive change at lightning speed is "to fit in and stand out."

Now, I want to share what I've learned with others.

Blythe J. McGarvie
Williamsburg, VA
January 2005

INTRODUCTION

If I were to place an ad for readers for this book, it would say:

Wanted: Aspiring Leaders

Recent college graduates and businesspeople ready for the fast track, middle managers anxious to advance, executives aiming for the C-suite or the boardroom, and any employee who wants to improve team performance. Willingness to contribute, active mind, high energy, and ambition required.

If you fit the profile in my ad, this book is a worthwhile employment of your capital and your time. It is the book that I wish someone had handed me at the beginning of my career. I wished for a leadership book that would open the door to the C-suite (the chief executive team), that offered advice from leaders who had "been there and done that," that was firmly grounded in reality, and that explained how to judge and act on the contradictory demands that constantly challenge senior executives. It is a street-smart guide to corporate and career success. As you will see, growth and achievement of goals in one's company and in one's own personal success go hand in hand for the FISO Factor leader. These goals can and should be accomplished simultaneously.

The theme of the book is straightforward and will be unsurprising to already successful leaders. But, perhaps because it is derived from practical experience, it is largely unrecognized in the literature on leadership. Simply stated, successful leadership is powered by two imperatives: fitting-in and standing-out. These imperatives are the FISO Factor.

Any aspiring leader who is pursuing a career in business is familiar with the first imperative. Business is a group endeavor. Your ability as a leader to fit into the group and to create a cohesive group that can work effectively toward shared goals are necessities of corporate and career success. Even the most powerful leaders must fit in; otherwise, their constituents may not chose to follow them. At the same time, aspiring leaders must stand out from the group to be recognized and followed, and to drive corporate change and growth. No matter what style of leadership you embrace—the humble servant, the charismatic dictator, or any in-between style—to be an effective leader, you must provide a beacon for others to follow.

You must fit in and stand out. These are two opposing concepts and they appear to embody a contradiction. Doesn't it follow that the more you stand out, the less you fit in, and vice versa? If you are better at one, don't you automatically become worse at the other? Clearly, the oppositional nature of the two imperatives complicates the leadership journey. I believe it also explains why so few aspiring leaders create the levels of performance they envision for their companies and reach their ultimate career goals. If not mastered, the imperatives of fitting-in and standing-out become barriers in their leadership journeys and block success.

The mandatory, but contradictory, demand that leaders be masters at both fitting-in and standing-out is a conundrum that I have studied and grappled with throughout my business career. Twenty-seven years ago, as a young associate at Arthur Andersen, I needed to fit in and stand out to establish a position in the competitive world of the Big Eight accounting firms. As a manager and executive at Kraft Foods, Inc., and Sara Lee Corporation, I needed to fit in and stand out to hit performance targets and move through the ranks of management. As CFO of Fortune 500 Hannaford Bros Co. and international consumer products company Société BIC, I had to fit in and stand out at the C-level. Today, perhaps more than ever, as a speaker, consultant, and a director on corporate boards, including Accenture, Pepsi Bottling Group, St. Paul Travelers, Wawa, and Lafarge NA, I find myself continually required to meet these dual imperatives.

Of course, I did not solve this puzzle on my own. I have been lucky to benefit from the insights of the many successful leaders I have worked for, worked with, and met over the past years. Their examples and their advice have been instrumental in what you will read here. The work of leadership experts, consultants, and academics are also an integral part of this book. I've let all of them speak for themselves whenever possible.

The purpose of this book is to offer you a viable means for resolving for yourself the inherent contradiction between fitting-in and standing-out. It will show you how to develop your FISO Factor level by exploring the six elements, catalytic agents, which support both imperatives simultaneously. Further, it will show you how to utilize the FISO Factor to build greater levels of corporate performance and the career success that accompanies it. In other words, you will help your business entity succeed and enjoy your own personal success.

Toward these ends, the book begins with three chapters that unlock the door of the C-Suite and reveal how senior business leaders approach their work. You cannot become a better leader until you have a clear notion of what leaders do.

The first chapter, The Everyday Work of Leaders, describes the current leadership environment, explains the relationship between corporate and career success, and introduces the two imperatives of corporate success. The second chapter, Fit In and Stand Out, concentrates on the individual's aspirations and leadership skills by describing the two career imperatives of the FISO Factor and their relationship to the corporate essentials. Chapter 3, The Catalytic Agents of the FISO Factor, offers the first view of how you can solve the FISO dilemma. It introduces the six catalytic agents that power both fitting-in and standing-out, and comprise the ever-rising platform on which you can build your leadership success.

Chapters 4 through 9, the heart of the book and the bulk of its content, explore the six catalysts and their roles in releasing the leader within. Each of these six chapters is devoted to a single catalyst, explaining what it is, why it works, and how it works. The career and the corporate applications of each catalyst are described. After all, leadership success requires corporate as well as individual career success. Each of these chapters ends with an "ABCs" (attitudes, behaviors, and characteristics) worksheet that you can use to begin building your mastery of the catalysts.

- Chapter 4, "Financial Acuity: The Language of Business," describes the financial savvy that is the basis of the business leadership platform. The foundational agent of FISO is financial acuity because without it, you cannot comprehend and, indeed, cannot survive in today's business world.
- Chapter 5, "Integrity: The Leader's North Star," describes a quality whose recent absence in a few conspicuous instances, has

tarred the reputation of all business leaders. Organizational and individual integrity direct and temper every decision leaders make and every action they take.

- Chapter 6, "Linkages: The Lever of Alliance," describes the nature and value of the individual connections between people that form a leader's network. Linkages are the pathways that provide leaders access to resources.

- Chapter7, "Learning: The Wellspring of Renewal," describes the most critical element in the continued growth of a business. Learning enables leaders and their companies to respond and adapt to their ever-changing environments.

- Chapter 8, "Perspective: The Prism of Insight," describes the substantial, but often ignored, role that perspective plays in leadership. Other people's perspectives enhance a leader's decision making and his or her ability to garner and mobilize support.

- Chapter 9, "Global Citizenship: The Passport to Opportunity," describes the exponential increase in corporate and career success that derives from globalization. Global citizenship enables leaders to transcend geographical boundaries in the quest for markets, as well as in the search for linkages, learning, and perspectives.

In the book's epilogue, "Choosing Your Path," we pull all these threads together and explore two last practical issues: when and where to best apply and develop your FISO Factor capabilities. In this concluding section, you will gain some insight into how to see the signs and pinpoint the most promising venues for applying your new skills and capabilities.

One final note before we embark on this voyage: Throughout my career and no matter what the current economic conditions and climate, the forecast for leadership effectiveness and success has never varied all that much. It usually sounds like this: There is plenty of leadership potential on the horizon, but only a small percentage of that potential develops and reaches the companies that need it so badly. *Fit In, Stand Out* is my effort to show effective leadership can shine on your company and in your life. Knowing what you need to do for success is only the beginning; let us also have fun doing it.

FIT IN, STAND OUT

THE EVERYDAY WORK
OF LEADERS

Perceptions about leadership opportunities tend to vary with our positions. To those at the entry level, the opportunities to become a leader are exciting but impossibly far away. For middle managers, after a number of years and successes, the C-suite is within eyesight, but the path still is not obvious. Finally, executives and board members who are charged with filling leadership positions may perceive that the opportunities to do some leading are abundant, but wonder how to about the task? Having experienced the business world at each level, I subscribe to this: There is plenty of room at the top.

There is, in fact, an urgent need for leaders. In spite of the recent turmoil caused by economic cycles, which seemed to have suddenly burst, and financial scandals, Horatio Alger lives, not just in old dime novels but in today's real world, too. The opportunities available for leaders in our capitalist economy, which increasingly has come to be synonymous with the global economy, are virtually limitless.

Of course, by the very structure of the corporate pyramid, top leadership positions seem scarce in comparison to the openings at lower levels. There are an estimated 15 million supervisors and middle managers in North America, 20 times the number of C-level executives. It is obvious that there cannot be room for everyone at the top and yet, it bears repeating that there is plenty of room for leaders who can demonstrate their effectiveness.

Consider the retained executive search industry, for example, which is only one small part of the leadership landscape. Even through a tender economic cycle, retained search firms in 2003 earned approximately $2 billion from companies in hot pursuit of capable leaders. These search firms employed over 13,000 recruiters in North America in 2003. A single CFO at Hannaford Bros. Co., the Fortune 500 supermarket retailer, logged 67 calls from retained search firms—almost one per week through an 18-month period ending in June 1999. If leadership opportunities were scarce, one would hardly expect to see this level of demand.

Empirical research further supports the anecdotal evidence that good leaders are difficult to find. In 2002, for instance, The Conference Board reported:

> In 1997, about half of the respondents to a Conference Board survey rated their company's leadership strength as either excellent or good. In 2001, however, only about a third of respondents rated their company's leadership capacity to meet business challenges or to respond to sudden change as excellent or good.

Developmental Dimensions International (DDI), a Pittsburgh, PA-based human resources consultancy, has been measuring leadership scarcity biannually since in 1999. In its 2003–2004 Leadership

Forecast, the firm reported: "While economic conditions in 2003 may be tough and many people are looking for jobs, scarcity of leadership talent remains a critical issue." In 1999, 74 percent of survey respondents reported that finding leadership candidates was somewhat or very difficult. In 2001, the figure jumped to 82 percent. In 2003, it eased slightly to 78 percent. Thus, even with the availability of former Internet companies' management after the bust of the dot-com rage, roughly three-quarters of respondents, from private and public companies located in 14 countries and with over 1,000 employees, say they have trouble filling their leadership opportunities. Further DDI reports that fully half of the organizations surveyed expect that it will become "either more difficult or much more difficult to find qualified candidates in the future."

The tremendous increases in executive compensation provide a final piece of evidence of the paucity of leaders. Controversy rages over the size of the pay packages currently being awarded to leaders of major companies. Many observers point to this as a sign of greed and corruption. The truth is quite the opposite. The prevailing image of a Corporate America beset by executives who are milking companies for personal gain is flat wrong. The reality is that the demand for leadership is perennially high, and high demand and low supply yield higher compensation. This is a basic tenet of our economic system: It is leaders who are the scarce commodity, not leadership positions. This begs the question: If there is no actual shortage of leadership opportunity, why does moving up the corporate ladder appear so difficult to so many?

AMBITIOUS, BUT UNPREPARED

Some people self-select out of business because they do not have the fortitude, smarts, or attitude for the work, preparing the way for those who are willing to learn the secrets for success. Ambition thrives in the hearts and minds of many and belies the often-given reason for the leadership shortage. I speak to and work with a wide variety of groups and repeatedly hear the same questions from college and graduate students, frontline employees, operational managers, and even executives who have already achieved a significant measure of success. They want to know how to start their careers on a fast track, leap the chasm between middle management and senior leadership, break through the glass ceiling and other limitations to success, and become leadership prospects demanded by corporate officers. They want to scale the heights.

While their ambition is inner-driven, it is generally neither inner-directed nor unbridled. I do not hear undertones of the grasping pursuit of personal power and gain that too often becomes the lead story in the business news. Over the decades, films and books often conjured the image of the successful businessperson as a robber baron or heartless greedy megalomaniac. Certainly, John D. Rockefeller would have no truck with that kind of ambition. A no-nonsense businessperson who built Standard Oil Company into a colossus, Rockefeller created one of America's greatest family fortunes. In 1909, he also wrote these still-relevant words:

> If I were to give advice to a young man starting out in life, I
> should say to him: If you aim for a large, broad-scaled success,
> do not begin your business career, whether you sell your labor
> or are an independent producer, with the idea of getting from
> the world by hook or crook all you can. . . .The man will be the
> most successful who confers the greatest service on the world.

People not only increase their productivity, but also experience joy as a result of their tempered, value-directed ambition. I hear it often as aspiring leaders talk about wanting to build companies that are responsible to their customers, employees, and their communities, as well as

4

their shareholders; that create products and services designed to improve the human condition; that create value and wealth for all of their stakeholders. Rockefeller advocated this kind of ambition.

If ambition alone provided all that was required to become a leader, there would be no shortage of leaders. But it isn't. Aspiring leaders must know when, where, and how to direct their efforts. Once they get inside a company, they must successfully figure out which choices to make, who to emulate and trust, and how to identify and unlock the right doors. This is no simple task. With each position, I developed; it struck me that I would be opening several doors and closing a few options. For example, when I decided to leave a brand management position for a corporate finance position at one of my companies, I knew that it would be virtually impossible to ever rejoin the marketing side of the business. On the other hand, the new position included managing the worldwide annual budgeting on which all management bonuses depended. This responsibility opened many doors for me to learn the strategies and plans of a multiple of divisions and functions.

Employers try to help. After all, they are urgently concerned with developing a robust and qualified pool of leadership candidates. American companies spend heavily on leadership development; in total, they spent $26.3 billion on management and executive education in 2004. Training and its successful adaptation and application, however, are two very different things. Ultimately, aspiring leaders must leave the theoretical and peaceful environment of the classroom and apply what they have learned in the workplace. In the workplace, never-ending demands and chaotic change rule the day. This is where many lose their bearings and where the leadership shortage is rooted.

Too many aspiring leaders never become adept at navigating within their organizations. They are often well educated and their companies provide copious amounts of technical training, so they tend to have the fundamental managerial skills. However, they are mentally unprepared for the rigors and realities of leadership.

This lack of preparation is sure to become even more critical in the future. The same Conference Board study quoted above looked ahead to 2010. It compiled the folowing list of ten attributes that leaders will have to possess to be successful in the future:

- Cognitive ability—both raw "intellectual horsepower" and mental agility
- Strategic thinking skills, especially with regard to global competition and the application of technology
- Analytical ability, especially the ability to sort through information sources and focus on the most relevant aspects
- The ability to make sound decisions in an environment of ambiguity and uncertainty
- Personal and organizational communication skills
- Influence and persuasion within the organization as well as with customers, suppliers, strategic partners, external constituents, and investors
- The ability to manage in an environment of diversity— this includes not only managing across cultures in a global workplace, but employing a variety of management styles to deal with multiple generations in the workplace
- The ability to delegate tasks and responsibilities to others, while at the same time managing risk and establishing appropriate controls
- The ability to identify, attract, develop, and retain talent at all levels
- Personal adaptability—the ability to learn from experience and adjust course appropriately

Taken in one gulp, these attributes might be tough for even the most ambitious aspiring leader to swallow. But it is not as overwhelming as it first appears. In fact, my purpose in this book is to offer advice and specific tools that encompass a framework for developing these skills. It is designed for ambitious businesspeople who wish to prepare themselves to lead. Further, I address leadership preparation from the practical, street-smart perspective of leaders who have "been there and done that." My aim is twofold: to offer a plainspoken and accurate understanding of the roles that leaders play in business organizations and to describe the fundamental "ABCs"—attitudes, behaviors, and characteristics—that enable leaders to effectively fulfill their roles.

OFTEN FORGOTTEN PRECEPTS

There are two precepts that should inform and guide aspiring leaders in their approach to their work. You might think them obvious. Yet, if so, why are they so often forgotten or ignored?

Leadership success is synonymous with organizational success is the first precept. Over the years, I have read a good number of books that promised to reveal the secrets of leadership success and then focused almost entirely on personal career strategies. These books, which often advocate political maneuver, aggressive self-promotion, and cutthroat competition instead of the creation and maintenance of healthy businesses, subvert the very definition of leadership.

One result of this subversion is clearly evident in the shocking proliferation of financial scandals in the past few years—Enron, WorldCom, and Tyco, to name a few. An undue focus on short-term results and share price is often blamed for these scandals. Certainly, responsibilities to shareholders have increased in recent decades due to changes in corporate laws, the increase in investment opportunities and money managers, and the greater availability of data through the Internet. "Market pressure," we are told, has caused good leaders to do bad things. This is a red herring. It is more likely that the leaders of these companies were focused solely on maximizing their personal gains.

7

Parmalat, the global dairy food giant and, until recently, one of Italy's blue-chip corporations, demonstrates what happens when personal interests take precedence over long-term corporate interests for an extended period. Over a 15-year period, the company's managers, who under the control of the Tanzi family, systematically invented assets in order to disguise the depth of the company's liabilities. On December 30, 2003, three days after the $9.2 billion company declared bankruptcy, its founder and CEO Calisto Tanzi admitted that the books had been cooked to the tune of $10 billion. The Italian government's prosecutors allege that Tanzi diverted as much as $990 million of that amount for his own use.

Stories like this offer an important lesson to aspiring leaders. It is that their career success is intimately tied to the long-term success of their organizations. They must also realize that the long-term interests of their companies can coexist in harmony with their individual interests.

Corporate success, and thus leadership success, is measured financially is the second precept. No matter what vision and values a corporation chooses to adopt, its lifeblood is money. Money funds its operations and its growth. Making money is a leader's job.

Surprisingly, leaders sometimes seem to forget that they are in business to earn money. They confuse the means by which a company creates its income stream and profits with its ends. Strategies, such as innovation, are means of earning profits; they are not, in and of themselves, business ends.

Apple Computer provides an interesting example of this phenomenon. Apple is a paragon of innovation. It virtually founded the personal computer industry and first commercialized a long list of digital goodies, including the mouse, the laser printer, the color monitor, and the PDA (remember Newton?). Most recently, with iTunes and iPod, the company successfully established the first sustainable business model for the online music industry. Steve Jobs, the company's leader and champion of some of its greatest products, is justly proud of his company's accomplishments. "Innovate. That's what we do," he declared in 2003 at Apple Expo in Paris.

There is a dark side to this picture, however. *Fast Company* recently reported that for all of Apple's innovation prowess, in 2003, the company held just 2 percent of the $180 billion global market for PCs. It ranked ninth among PC makers, and its profit margins are 0.4%, one-fifth of the industry average. One reason for this might be that for all his business genius, Jobs mistakenly views innovation as an end instead of a means to an end. The end is revenue growth and profitability, and Jobs often appears to deemphasize that basic lesson of business leadership. No matter what strategy a business leader conceives and pursues, it must ultimately be capable of creating profits.

LEADERS ARE SYSTEMS THINKERS

Once aspiring leaders understand the correct basis for career success, they can attack the question of how to accomplish that goal. Career success first and foremost depends on the financial foundation of the company's success and some good luck. Unfortunately, luck may seem out of your hand and dependent on a unique time in history. Yet, successful individuals thrive in any period, creating conflicting answers to this question. And, to make matters more confusing, the answers appear to change over time.

How do you accomplish successful results in your company and for the shareholder? Product and service quality, for instance, was considered the correct answer in the 1980s and early 1990s. Reengineering had its run in the mid-1990s. E-business was the rage until early 2001. Lately, there seem to be a variety of concepts—innovation, six sigma, balanced scorecards, and outsourcing to name a few—that are driving competing strategic paradigms. Which is the right answer? All of them are . . . to some degree.

A better way to approach this question is to step back and examine the leader's work from a distance and as a whole. Sometimes I feel as if I've been struggling to decipher the code of organizational success forever. I studied it in undergraduate and postgraduate classes; practiced it as an executive in a variety of corporations and many different countries; honed it in the C-suite in several billion-dollar companies; in recent years, I've overseen it from the boardroom, taught it as a consultant, and preached it as a speaker. One of the most important lessons I've learned is that systems are the primary determinants of outcomes.

This lesson made management thinkers such as W. Edwards Deming and Peter Senge famous, and rightly so. Deming's Red Bead Experiment was a striking illustration of the need to take a systems-based approach to quality for manufacturers around the world. He would provide a box filled with 4,000 wooden beads (80 percent white and 20 percent red), give seminar participants a paddle for scooping the beads, and instruct them to pick up only white beads. He would praise, reward, and threaten to try to get them to produce defect-free work (scoops with no red beads). But, of course, it was virtually impossible to scoop only white beads. The lesson: Systems create performance boundaries, and the only way to exceed those boundaries is to redesign the system.

Peter Senge, who introduced the concept of the "learning organization" with his seminal book, *The Fifth Discipline*, is also a dedicated advocate of developing and implementing proper systems thinking as a means of improving performance. In fact, he identifies systems thinking as the most important of the five components or "disciplines" that create, fuel, and foster a learning organization, saying, "It is the discipline that integrates the disciplines, fusing them into a coherent body of theory and practice."

Senge found that systems thinking is indispensable because it enables us to understand the growing complexity of our companies and effectively shape them. "Systems thinking," he writes, "is a discipline for seeing wholes. It is a framework for seeing interrelationships rather than things, for seeing patterns of change rather than static 'snapshots.'" Further, it allows leaders to understand the often far-flung effects of their actions and build companies that are greater than the sums of their parts.

So, aspiring leaders need to approach their companies from a holistic, systems perspective. Their effectiveness and the organizational performance and career success that derive from it are subject to this principle. If you wish to maximum your impact on your company's performance, you must take a systems approach. Without it, you will have only an episodic or random effect on the circumstances confronting you. An internal framework that becomes part of your mental DNA and allows you to respond quickly and instinctively will become the guideline for your conscience and ambition.

THE TWO IMPERATIVES OF A DYNAMIC BUSINESS SYSTEM

On the surface, individual companies or "corporate systems" do not appear to have much in common. To be sure, every company is unique and its specific framework and processes vary widely. But in my experience, the generation of sustainable shareholder value and employee success in any company can be distilled down to two imperatives: integration and transformation. These are the two forces that power the essential dynamic of all business systems.

- *Integration is the force behind standardization, stability, and economy*. Integration enables all of the disparate elements of a company to fit together, work efficiently, and maximize profit. When companies standardize their product offerings, connect information systems, and cross-sell to existing customers, they are pursuing the integration imperative.

11

- *Transformation is the force behind differentiation and change.* Transformation enables a company to set itself apart from its competitors and create new growth engines. When companies produce innovative new products and services, enter new markets, and adopt new skills and competencies, they are pursuing the transformation imperative.

I realize that the idea that a system as complex as a global corporation can be reduced to the interplay between just two forces might sound improbable. But, there is evidence that supports the idea. First, significant historical precedent provides the foundation for this perspective. For over two thousand years, philosophers in the Far East have described the world as being driven by two forces, *yin* and *yang*. (See the sidebar.) I see the imperatives of integration and transformation as the yin and yang of business.

There are strong echoes of the concept of yin and yang in business, especially when the merging and balancing of elements that would appear on the surface to be contradictory has lead to important breakthroughs. The concept of mass customization, creating one-of-kind products in a large-scale manufacturing environment, is one example. Another is one-to-one marketing, the idea of sending individually targeted messages to hundreds of thousands of customers at once. The human dynamics and the scientific discoveries over the centuries can be understood to work together. You do not have to choose one or the other, but must incorporate both forces.

YIN AND YANG

The concepts of yin and yang first appeared in China roughly two hundred years before the birth of Christ. During the early Han Dynasty, ambitious Chinese scholars attempted to merge the ideas of several prominent, but rival philosophers, including Confucius, Lao Tzu, and Mo Tzu, into a single, unified philosophical system. In this process, they added an appendix to the ancient Chinese text I Ching (Book of Changes) designed to explain the mechanism that powered the entire universe.

The central dynamic of the universe, according to the Han philosophers, is driven by two opposing forces, the yin and the yang. They said that everything in our world—politics, the environment, human health, business, etc.—is given form and definition by these two forces. The yin is a negative force; the yang a positive one. They are value neutral, that is, neither is good or bad. In fact, they work together and balance each other to create a harmonious universe. These two opposing elements define the system and complement, rather than contradict, one another.

Two thousand years later, the scientific method has replaced the I Ching as a means to understand the world in most quarters. But, the concepts of yin and yang resonate in me whenever I attempt to explain the nature of organizations to aspiring leaders. You can understand and manage your organization by thinking of it in terms of the interaction between the two opposing imperatives of integration and transformation.

Furthermore, the myriad strategies of business are all aimed at integration, transformation, or both imperatives simultaneously. In the chapters describing the six critical agents, I will show when and how each imperative evolves with the increasing complexity of business. Sometimes this is obvious. For example, innovation, when it is aimed at producing new products, services, or business models, is usually a force of transformation. On the other hand, reengineering, when it is used to redesign work processes to better connect functions and improve work flow, is aimed at enhancing integration. These and other strategies can also encompass both imperatives at once. Learning initiatives, depending on their goal, often have both integrative and transformational results. Thus, when a company better educates its employees, it can simultaneously improve its level of integration and create a more effective platform for developing breakthroughs in innovation. Likewise, a well-conceived corporate merger can better integrate a company to deal with existing customer demands and at the same time transform it through access to new markets.

Just as the philosophers of the Han Dynasty saw a universe dependent on the interplay of the yin and yang, companies are dependent on the interplay between the imperatives of integration and transformation. No company can be successful in the long term by pursuing only one imperative or the other. Both forces must be present.

This is an important insight. The leader who focuses only on integration will never reach beyond its existing boundaries. As the market moves past the company, it is destined for obsolescence. The often-heard example is the buggy whip manufacturer that concentrates on making the best buggy whips in the world. Its leaders concentrate on integrative initiatives—improving quality, building production efficiency, and lowering costs. But when the market for buggy whips disappears, these efforts make little difference and the company disappears too.

AT&T has been struggling with this conundrum for over a decade. After the company was ordered to divest its regional local service businesses by the U.S. Department of Justice in 1984, its cash cow was residential long-distance telephone service, a partially regulated market. With the passage of the 1996 Telecommunications Act, long distance was deregulated. The Baby Bells, as well as a host of other competitors, entered the market. Prices plummeted.

Faced with the loss of his company's core business, CEO and chairman Robert Allen chose to take an integrative approach. He competed

14

head-to-head and unsuccessfully attempted to create a more compelling bundle of telephony services for customers by merging with a large local service provider. But like the buggy whip maker, these efforts did not address the larger issue: competition was squeezing all of the profits out of long distance. (This condition was exacerbated by MCI WorldCom's fraudulent accounting, which covered up the fact that that company was selling long distance at a loss and by some estimates, cost AT&T $5 billion per year as it lowered prices to remain competitive.)

After several more leadership missteps, AT&T hired Michael Armstrong as its chairman and CEO in late 1997. Armstrong leaped into the work of transformation. He raced to establish new businesses with the dwindling profits from long distance. But, the crash of the financial markets in 2001 stymied his plan before its fruition. He did, however, save AT&T from the ultimate loss; by 2002, eight of AT&T's largest eleven competitors had declared bankruptcy. AT&T, by the way, is currently withdrawing from the residential local and long distance markets. In June 2004, it announced it would stop competing for that business in seven states comprising 38 million customers because it "will likely be unable to economically serve customers with the competitive bundles currently available."

A singular focus on transformation can be just as dangerous. Tom Kelley, the founder of international design firm IDEO, says, "No one gets ahead by copying the status quo." He is right; transformational breakthroughs are necessary. But, the company that focuses only on transformation never establishes a secure position in the marketplace. It is destined to always chase the promise of future profits, but never achieve the full potential of its efforts. As we have seen, this is a problem that plagues Apple Computer. Too often, other companies have ended up owning the markets it pioneered.

The rush for Internet gold, a seemingly infinite vein of ore that abruptly petered out in early 2001, provides many examples of companies that were all transformation and no integration. There was a company called Digiscent that raised $20 million in funding to launch a digital product called iSmell that was designed to add scent to Web sites. Another Internet company named Flooz.com raised over $51 million in funding to sell alternative money to online shoppers. The list goes on and on.

The Internet craze was so pervasive that solid "Old Economy" companies fell into disrepute. The stock price of what many consider the ultimate blue chip, Warren Buffet's Berkshire Hathaway, fell 50 percent in 1999. Of course, Berkshire Hathaway recovered all of its value and much more. Meanwhile, a vast majority of the Internet companies, including Flooz.com and Digiscent, that promised to transform the face of business now exist in memory only.

The important point is that successful business systems require both integration and transformation. The everyday work of leaders is to recognize and manage the two imperatives of business systems. A leader's personal success is merely a by-product of that work.

2

FIT IN *AND* STAND OUT

I meet far too many businesspeople whose career paths have become cycles of frustration. They feel mired in their current positions. When they try to move forward, they cannot find firm footing or make any meaningful progress. They struggle to contribute to their organizations, but are unsure of how to act effectively. They remind me of Alice and her trip to Wonderland.

In 1865, an Oxford mathematician named Charles Lutwidge Dodson self-published a flight of fancy that has entranced both children and adults ever since. Writing as Lewis Carroll, Dodson created an excellent parable for all aspiring leaders. As you may recall, in *Alice's Adventures in Wonderland*, Lewis Carroll's eponymous heroine falls down a rabbit hole into a world where fractured logic, paradox, and contradiction rule the day. Alice's goal is clear: she just wants to go home. But, her journey through Wonderland is filled with obstacles. She is unable to move about freely in this dream world. By turn, she is too tall to fit through doors, too short to reach the keys for locks; so small that she almost drowns in her own tears, so big that she fills a house to the point of serious injury. She asks the bizarre residents of Wonderland for help, but cannot make sense of their advice. She cannot understand the rules that govern behavior in this world and almost loses her head.

The work world can seem a lot like Wonderland. At work your goals are clear: to deliver service to your employer; to add value to your company; and to earn your salary. But how? Like Alice, aspiring leaders are often unable to find the doors to the right opportunities. When they finally locate the right doors, they find they can't fit through them—they don't have the necessary attitudes, behaviors, or characteristics. They work hard and acquire these attributes only to find that, like Alice, their keys have disappeared—often, the environment has changed or the opportunity is no longer a viable option. Eventually, like Alice, they might cross the thresholds of new opportunities only to find themselves in even more incomprehensible situations.

The consequences of this cycle of frustration can be costly. Unlike Alice's dream, a career in business is real. Those who struggle fruitlessly become more and more likely to give up completely. They find that they are unable to contribute to the success of their companies and their careers stall. Both the aspiring leaders and their organizations suffer.

NAVIGATING THROUGH THE CORPORATE WONDERLAND

If future and current leaders equip themselves properly, their career paths do not have to be painful slogs. With the right attitudes, behaviors, and characteristics, they can successfully navigate the corporate wonderland and create corporate and career success. We've already discussed in the first chapter the corporate component of career navigation: would-be leaders must understand the symbiotic relationship between corporate and career success, the financial essence of a business, and the yin and yang of corporate success. But that knowledge is organizational in nature—it is focused on your company. It is only half of the leadership equation.

Leadership effectiveness also has a personal component, an individual aspect that is as important as its organizational aspect. The second half of the leadership equation is about managing yourself. It is about the creation of a personal platform for leadership.

We often hear about platforms in relation to the positions of political candidates and parties. In business, we also talk about platforms in relation to the development of software and product lines. Leaders have platforms, too. A leader's platform is the stage from which she directs and furthers her organization's growth. The most important component of this platform is your values and actions. It also encompasses your experience, your accomplishments, your resources, and your ability to help others and have them help you.

When constructed properly, this personal platform provides stability and support because it is built upon and directly connected to the energy and resources of the entire organization. At the same time, this platform provides visibility and authority because it extends above the organization and defines purpose and direction.

Knowing that leadership success is synonymous with corporate success, it should come as little surprise when I state that the creation of a secure and visible leadership platform is ruled by the same essential interplay between the imperatives of integration and transformation as a business system. A leadership platform is anchored through the integrative process and its visibility is established through the transformational process. To put this in terms of your career path, integration is the process of "fitting-in" and transformation is the process of "standing-out."

Fitting-in is the process of integrating oneself into the culture and structure of a company. It is discovering the way in which things get done and establishing oneself as a team player. A team player is someone who seeks to achieve group objectives; who can be depended upon; and who brings valued skills and attitudes to the group. To "fit in" also refers to your ability to support, maintain, and work within the system.

Standing-out is the process of developing the visibility one needs to advance within the system. It is knowing how and when to take the lead, how and when to undertake change, and how and when to provide the impetus needed to grow the organization. No progress can occur without this ability. No significant achievements or rewards can be obtained without this ability. No dreams can be fulfilled without this ability. To "stand out" also refers to your ability to transform the system itself and help it grow beyond its established boundaries.

Just as integration and transformation are the imperatives of corporate success, fitting-in and standing-out are the imperatives of career success.

FITTING-IN

Fitting-in is a task that each of us undertakes throughout our lives as we attempt to integrate with society at large. Our parents begin this process when we are babies by teaching us the skills we need to fit into the world. As teenagers, we struggle with the dictates of peer pressure. As adults, we try to make a place for ourselves within our own families and our communities. Fitting-in plays the same integrative role in our work lives.

When you enter a company and begin the process of fitting-in, you are demonstrating that you understand and accept the norms of the organization. You show that you are not a threat to the people around you and that you can empathize with their situations. You build trust and attract support as a team player. You begin to establish a secure foundation for your leadership platform.

MY FATHER'S PHD

Your career path often becomes blocked when you do not fit in. This is a point that was driven home for me after my father, Ernest Jaski, died at the age of 79. My father taught for three decades in the City Colleges of Chicago. Over the years he initiated many wonderful educational programs. For instance, he taught English as a second language to Vietnamese and Cambodian refugees and found over 600 jobs for his students. *The Chicago Tribune* published his obituary under the headline: *"City Colleges educator devoted career to his love of learning."*

Don, a friend of my father, drove three hours to attend the funeral and tell us a story dating back 40 years. One day in the early 1960s, Don, two other students, and my father defended their dissertations, the final step to their doctorates, at the University of Chicago. A week later, Don learned that all but my father had passed their oral interrogations. He was incredulous and asked the adviser of the doctorate committee, "How could this be? Ernest is the brightest, worked the hardest, and clearly deserves the degree as much as any of us. It doesn't make sense." The adviser replied that the committee had felt that Ernest was "not the type of person they wanted representing the University." The adviser said my father, whose parents were Polish immigrants and who came from a working-class background, tried too hard. He was always rushing around with his shirttail out. (My father was working two jobs to support us while he was working toward his doctorate.)

This was "not quite the image" of a University of Chicago PhD, said the adviser.

My family knew that my father applied for his doctorate repeatedly. It was a topic of much discussion between him and my mother, but we had not known the reason why. My father never quit and in June 1969, after eight years, he earned his PhD. I guess the committee ran out of excuses.

There are a couple of lessons here. One is certainly the power of persistence, a lesson my father taught us well. The other can be found in the obstacles that my father was forced to overcome because he did not appear to fit in. I think that we should all be true to ourselves and proud of our heritages, but if we want to become productive and accepted members of an organization and work effectively within it, we should be willing to conform to its standards within the boundaries of our integrity and values.

Fitting-in is not just a matter of getting in. The higher you climb up the ladder of leadership responsibility, the more important it becomes. Many people who work within companies think of their leaders as omnipotent. Leaders' orders come down from above and everyone starts marching. This is, however, an oversimplified and inaccurate portrait of executive authority. In fact, business leaders cannot be effective unless they fit in, that is, until others accept them as leaders. They know, or soon discover, that they cannot lead if they have no followers.

Ronald Heifetz, professor at Harvard's Kennedy School of Government and cofounder of the Center for Public Leadership, explains this reality very well:

I define authority as conferred power to perform a service. This definition will be useful to the practitioner of leadership as a reminder of two facts: First, authority is given and can be taken away. Second, authority is conferred as part of an exchange. Failure to meet the terms of exchange means the risk of losing one's authority: It can be taken back or given to another who promises to fulfill the bargain.

No matter where you are on the leadership hierarchy, you must recognize that followers grant authority only to those who exhibit superlative leadership skills and talents. In the wonderland of business, I have always tried to hire managers and executives who understood that authority is conferred and that they must fit into the existing organization before they could transform it. This is the only way to be an authentic contributor to an organization. I created the accompanying simple matrix to evaluate job candidates from this perspective.

Dispositions ↑	**Learners** *Hire and train, if feasible.*	**Leaders** *Hire and support relentlessly.*
	Losers *Dont hire or retain.*	**Lucifers** *Don't be seduced.*
	Skills →	

The axes on the matrix reflect the two questions that I would seek to answer before hiring a manager or anyone else for that matter. First, as reflected on the horizontal axis, does this person have the skills needed to do the job? Second, as reflected on the vertical axis, does this person have the disposition needed to fit into the corporate culture?

Candidates who score high on both questions are Leaders: They have skills and the disposition needed to succeed in your company.

Candidates who score low on both queries are Losers: They are non-starters who have neither the skills nor disposition needed to succeed. These are obvious, but what about candidates who fall into the remaining two sectors?

Candidates who score high on the disposition axis, but low on the skills axis are Learners. They can fit in if they have the capacity to acquire the needed skills; I would consider Learners as viable candidates. Candidates who score low on disposition and high on skills are another story altogether. I call them Lucifers because it is easy to get seduced by their promise. Lucifers often have impressive skills and resumes, but they do not fit in. Typically, they are poor hires.

As CFO of BIC, the French company that makes the familiar disposable pens and lighters, I hired a Lucifer. I found a candidate for a financial position who was highly skilled, but I did not spend enough time investigating her disposition. As it turned out, the door to her office was always closed and she did not like to communicate with her subordinates, peers, or me. She made little effort to fit into the existing culture at the company and as a result, could not play an effective role on the company's financial team. I tried to discuss these problems with her repeatedly; she continually asserted her technical competency. Within three months, we were having the formal, documented discussions required for termination in France. I had made a mistake and received a lower bonus payout as a direct result of hiring the employee.

The process of fitting-in helps establish the aspiring leader's credibility. Credibility, Jim Kouzes and Barry Posner argue in their book of the same name, is the cornerstone of leadership. Here's why, explains Kouzes:

> It can be stated in one sentence: if people don't believe in the messenger, they won't believe in the message. If you go to a bank for a line of credit, you fill out a credit application, and they do a credit check. Credit comes from the same root word

as credibility: credo. Credo is literally "I believe." The bank is checking to see if they should believe you. . . . Employees do the same thing. They look at their leaders and ask if they should believe them.

When leaders fit in, they gain credibility in the eyes of their followers. The quality of fitting-in offers one more essential leadership boost: It provides a secure foundation on which aspiring leaders can stand out.

STANDING-OUT

Fitting-in is essential to effective leadership, but it is not leadership's sole essence. You can conform to excess. You can blend in so well that you disappear into what one executive described to me as "the safety of the tall grass." I can see how the tall grass may appear to be a safe haven in the often-turbulent business world, but when the winds of change drive the periodic brushfires, it is not a good place to be hiding.

"Tall grass" sometimes manifests itself as excessive conformity. At other times, it is a reluctance to offer suggestions, resistance to change, or an overreliance on technical skills. It makes no difference in which guise it appears; managers who seek out the tall grass are putting their careers in jeopardy.

Quiet competence is not enough, either. How often do we hear people complain, "If only someone would recognize my potential, what I could do to improve things around here." Standing-out is not just about potential and achievement; it is also the willingness to *communicate* and *demonstrate* achievement. This is how you help others to recognize your potential.

George Dudley and the Behavior Sciences Research Press have conducted a series of studies on the psychology of reluctance—the hesitation to reach out to others and to stand out from others. They conducted one study in which the salary increases and promotions of administrative managers in a large company were tracked over five years. Dudley's conclusion:

> We found those who were promoted most often and given the biggest salary increases did not necessarily turn out to be those judged . . . to be the most technically competent. It was those who were most willing to make whatever level of competence they had *visible*.

Dudley's research team has replicated this finding in other studies. In one, CPAs who had been "out-placed" were compared with CPAs who had retained their jobs in the same organizations. Again, they found that those who lost their jobs were more hesitant to make their contributions visible.

Leadership requires visibility and visibility requires courage. Standing-out is an act that many people fear. It is one reason why surveys typically find that people fear public speaking more than they fear death itself. (Although I'm certain that anyone literally facing an immediate choice between giving a speech and death would choose the former.)

I think the quality of courage is so important to leaders that I have the word taped to my computer monitor where I can see it when I sit down to write. It takes courage to be different. It takes courage to embrace the career risk that is entailed in a public stand for a product or program or strategy. It takes courage to be in the point position that all effective leaders must assume. It also takes courage to risk revealing your vulnerabilities.

If you can muster that courage, how do you raise your visibility? In his book, *Thinking for a Living*, John Maxwell tells a story about Jack Welch, Fortune's "Manager of the Century." An audience member at one of Welch's speaking engagements asked him how to advance in a business world filled with ambitious people. Welch began by saying, "Great question, young man. And this is an important point for every person to hear. The first thing you must understand is the importance of getting out of 'the pile.'" He went on to advise the listeners to view every assignment they received from their bosses as an opportunity to get beyond the expected answers and add value to their companies. If they did, he said, they would get out of the pile fast.

Recently, I had the opportunity to ask GE's former leader about his answer. Welch told me, "I first learned that you must stand out when I was writing my thesis. That was when I realized that there was not one answer any longer. In school before that, I knew that the answers on the quiz would be the same answers I had heard in the lectures and read in the homework. But now, no one was telling me the right answer. I needed to think and work hard to get the best answer on my own."

Here is a good example of how to stand out. When I was CFO at Hannaford Bros. Co., the supermarket chain based in Maine, we thought that we could cut our costs if we took control of the financial switch that occurs when a customer pays by credit card, debit card, or personal check. (Usually a bank handles this part of the payment process and receives a fee in return.) I worked with a middle manager from IT named Steve on the project. Steve's job was to calculate the cost to run the financial switch ourselves.

When Steve presented his findings, however, we learned that he done more than that. In addition to calculating the costs, he analyzed the transactions and suggested ways in which we could entice our customers to use their debit cards, the least costly option for us to process. Steve showed us that we could increase our savings and our return on investment if we coupled the project with strategies that encouraged our customers to use their debit cards. He stood out. In fact, I offered him a promotion and a better paying job in the finance department shortly after he finished the project.

Although aspiring leaders must stand out in order to build successful careers, there are limits to this imperative. As with fitting-in, a sole focus on standing-out is ultimately a prescription for failure. Michael

Maccoby, who served as director of the program on technology, public policy, and human development at Harvard's Kennedy School of Government for over a decade, has studied the psychology of leaders who excel at standing-out. He calls these leaders "productive narcissists" and numbers corporate superstars such as Michael Dell, Andy Grove, and Jeff Bezos among them. In his McKinsey Award-winning *Harvard Business Review* article on the topic, Maccoby writes:

> Leaders such as Jack Welch or George Soros are examples of productive narcissists. They are gifted and creative strategists who see the big picture and find meaning in the risky proposition of changing the world and leaving behind a legacy. . . . Productive narcissists are not only risk takers willing to get the job done but also charmers who can convert the masses with their rhetoric.

Maccoby found a dark side to productive narcissists. They tend to be highly independent and often isolate themselves from others. They are sensitive to criticism, poor listeners, and overly competitive. They lack empathy and dislike mentoring others. Worse, their successes can tend to inflate their self-images and exacerbate their weaknesses. To paraphrase religious leader Ralph W. Sockman, the seeds of their defeat are sown along with their victories. If leaders recognize this vulnerability, they can change and continue to succeed. If not, they stand out too much and lose their ability to fit in.

It is easy to take pot shots at leaders such as "Chainsaw Al" Dunlap, whose concept of "mean business" resulted in the demise of Sunbeam, Tyco's Dennis Kozlowski, and Enron's Kenneth Lay after the fact, but I see them as examples of productive narcissists who succumbed to their weaknesses. I think their drive to stand out led them to ignore the boundaries of good business and the law. They offer a warning that we must heed. The degree to which an aspiring leader stands out and the methods he uses must always be tempered.

THE FISO FACTOR

Fitting-in and standing-out is the combination that enables successful leadership. They are the two elements that comprise the FISO Factor.

The FISO Factor—the principle of and skills for fitting-in and standing-out as an effective leader—is the key that unlocks the C-level suite. Many aspiring leaders are masters of one or the other element of FISO, but they cannot be successful in the long term by pursuing only one career imperative or the other. Those who are focused only on fitting-in will never get beyond the status quo. Their destiny is to be passed over again and again. Conversely, those who are focused only on standing-out will never establish the support required to succeed. Their destiny is to stand alone. To exert the highest degree of influence, successful leaders both fit in and stand out, and they understand how to anticipate and control the interplay between the two forces.

The ease with which you navigate your career path and the structural integrity of your leadership platform hinges on your ability to pursue these two contradictory imperatives of FISO. But, FISO is not like juggling on a tightrope.

You have to make choices, not juggle them. This distinction reminds me of a conversation that I had with the late Ruth Whitney, the legendary editor-in-chief of *Glamour* magazine. Ruth ran *Glamour* for 31 years. She was responsible for growing it into a highly successful women's magazine with a circulation of two million subscribers. Under her leadership, *Glamour* became the first major women's magazine to put an African-American model on its cover; it was also noted for covering controversial and serious women's issues, such as racism, abortion, and equal pay. Ruth led *Glamour* to two National Magazine Awards for General Excellence—the only women's magazine so honored.

The topic we discussed was the idea that the numbers of men and women in executive positions should be balanced to better reflect their proportional numbers in the population at large. Ruth was a dedicated mentor of women collegians, starting many on successful careers in publishing, but she objected to the word "balanced." She said, "Balance implies that you are juggling. What is really important is to recognize that there are *choices*." To Ruth, righting the gender inequities in the workplace was not about equal numbers, but expanded choices. She wanted employers to realize and act on the fact that women were viable candidates for executive positions, too.

Ruth also wanted women to realize they needed to make conscious and deliberate choices about how they spend their time and resources, that with these choices they established their priorities in life. If a woman made it a priority to focus on her professional success, that should be where her commitment, time, and ultimate success would also be. Ruth felt that too many women tried to do it all. In doing so, they dissipated their energies and ended up not doing anything really well.

The idea of choosing instead of juggling is a good way to think about developing and utilizing FISO. It is not a matter of evenly splitting your time between fitting-in and standing-out nor is there is any fixed ratio between the two imperatives. Rather, the key to FISO lies in the knowledge that both of its imperatives are requisites of successful leadership *and* in the ability to make informed choices between the two imperative based on corporate and career goals, the needs of the current situation, and the environment in which you must act.

I see elements of the FISO Factor in many of the lists of characteristics that aspiring leaders are asked to emulate and adopt. They are almost always combinations of the two qualities. The Boys and Girls Clubs of Chicago (BGCC), for which I served on the Corporate Board, provides an interesting example. BGCC endorses four critical elements—a sense of belonging, usefulness, competence, and influence—that build self-esteem in young people. A sense of belonging and usefulness addresses a child's need to fit in and become a productive member of his organizations and society. Competence and influence addresses a child's need to stand out, to be recognized for her unique talents, and to have a voice in her future. Together, these four elements add up to the FISO Factor.

I hope that, by now, I have convinced you of the compelling need to fit in and stand out in order to navigate the corporate wonderland and advance through the ranks of leadership. But there are many questions left to address, not the least of which is how do you develop and increase your FISO Factor? That is the question is the core of this book, and we will start to explore it in the next chapter.

3

THE CATALYTIC AGENTS
OF THE FISO FACTOR

Whether they realize it or not, great leaders develop and utilize the FISO Factor. They combine fitting-in and standing-out to form behavioral patterns that enable them to succeed. At the same time, they combine integration and transformation skills to enable their organizations to succeed also. Leaders who do this well seem to create results almost magically. Their work is a sort of leadership alchemy.

Mystics in Europe and the Middle East practiced alchemy for several thousand years up to about the seventeenth century. People today may envision alchemists as pointy-hatted wizards weaving spells in search of the philosopher's stone (reputedly capable of turning lead into gold) and the grand elixir of immortality. It is unfair, however, to evaluate alchemy outside the context of its time. Prior to the Scientific Revolution, mysticism was an integral and unquestioned part of human beliefs, so the mystical roots of alchemy are not so surprising. Alchemy was, in fact, the science of its day. The roots of modern medicine and chemistry can be traced back to the alchemists of medieval times. Alchemists pioneered the experimental precepts that later came to serve as the basis of the Scientific Method. It was Chinese alchemists who formulated black powder sometime around the ninth century.

The study of leadership itself contains more than a touch of alchemy. After all, there is no fixed periodic table of leadership elements, and the ways in which the ingredients of leadership are measured and mixed are mutable. We can ask followers what behaviors they want from their leaders and build models based on the responses. We can study the traits of successful leaders and attempt to create models based on their behavior. However, these models are theoretical constructs by definition, not guarantees of success. Further, even the best models are not flexible enough to contend with the multitude of ever-changing environments in which business leaders must act. Businesspeople who reach the highest levels of leadership must do so in an environment of constant change and exhibit the abilities to adapt to and anticipate market transformations.

Over the past fifty years CEOs have come from an increasingly varied functional background. After World War II, as the pent-up demand for goods exploded, production seeking to satisfy this demand became the driving force in many businesses. As a result, in the late 1940s and 1950s, CEOs tended to come from operational backgrounds. In the 1960s, competition grew and the ability to sell products became more critical. Accordingly, leadership candidates with sales backgrounds tended to rise to the top. In the 1970s, as competition continued to increase, marketing emerged as a critical discipline in business. At that time, marketers became the prime candidates to assume leadership positions. In the 1980s, industries consolidated and shareholder value became the raison d'etre in many companies. Corporate leaders tended to come from finance. In the mid-1990s, the "New Economy" emerged and CEOs tended to be technologists and venture capitalists. Today, we are in a period of flux in which CEOs must be generalists capable of responding to a variety of functional needs. And who can predict which functional skills will be in demand tomorrow?

As a leader, you cannot spend your time trying to predict every detail of an essentially unknowable future nor should you fruitlessly struggle to follow leadership models that cannot possibly take every situation into account. Instead, take a lesson from the alchemist: seek to identify and utilize the *catalysts* that enable a leader to respond to, create, and control change.

THE FISO FACTOR CATALYSTS

Scientists use catalysts to modify and increase the rate of chemical reactions. Typically, a formula consists of only a small amount of a catalyst relative to the reactants. The catalyst itself remains unchanged by the reaction. In broader terms, these powerful ingredients are agents capable of stimulating or precipitating a reaction, development, or change.

The FISO Factor also depends upon associated catalysts. These agents serve a dual purpose for the aspiring leader. First, they serve as building blocks of the FISO Factor itself. The more you practice and gain experience in different situations, the greater your awareness of when and how much you need to fit in or stand out. In other words, a leader's ability to fit in and stand out increases as her mastery of the catalysts grows. Second, they are tools that leaders can use to move their organizations. A leader's ability to integrate and transform his company grows along with his mastery of the catalysts.

There are six FISO Factor catalysts: financial acuity, integrity, linkages, learning, perspective, and global citizenship.

Financial Acuity

Finance is the language of business. You have certainly heard this statement before. It is the reason why academic classes in and books on "finance for nonfinancial managers" are perennially among the most popular in the field of business. I can also tell you from long experience as a financial professional that most aspiring leaders are simply not fluent in this language.

Further, financial fluency—the ability to read and speak the language of business—is not the only basis for true financial acuity. More important is the development of financial comprehension, that is, the ability to think about your company in the context of finance, to understand how your company makes money now, and how it could make money in the future.

THE KEY COMPONENT—FINANCIAL ACUITY

Give any of the following business scenarios a thorough consideration. You will find that financial acuity is the key component in the decision making and implementation.

- Running a marketing campaign: What's the payback? How much do we invest for what kind of return?
- Integrating a newly purchased company: What synergies and cost savings will result to ensure that the transaction will add value to the shareholders? How will we leverage the knowledge and technologies of the new company for revenue growth?
- Building a service component within a bricks-and-mortar company: Will this enhance our quality and therefore customer retention? How will we measure if we are effec-

tively investing resources (people, money, information) to build a lasting return on the investment?

More examples abound. To help you think through other scenarios, visit www.FISOFactor.com and develop your financial acuity.

Financial acuity should not be mistaken as accounting or simply "bean-counting." Steve Bollenbach was treasurer of Marriott Corporation in the 1980s and then assisted in the restructuring of Donald Trump's real estate empire. In 1992, when Bollenbach returned to Marriott as CFO, the company was in crisis. His success at Marriott demonstrates how financial acuity can be an important tool in the hands of a visionary manager. The story of how he helped transform Marriott is legendary.

Marriott had become a major hotel developer during the real estate boom of the 1980s. It had sold over $6 billion in properties and earned billions more in contracts for managing the properties. But in the late 1980s, real estate investors, particularly the Japanese, vanished and the hotel boom went bust. "We took a major hit on our stock price, had to lay off two entire departments of hard-working people, endured a brief takeover scare, and had the dubious pleasure of reading premature Marriott obituaries in the business media," recalled Chairman and CEO J.W. Marriott, Jr. Worse, the company had $2.9 billion in unsold properties and $1 billion in debt dragging it down.

It was Bollenbach who introduced the plan to split the company into two entities in order to revitalize its prospects. Marriott Corporation, which changed its name to Host Marriott, kept the properties and the debt. The management business was spun off as Marriott International and was, as J.W. Marriott said, "virtually debt-free, giving it more flexibility to go after management contracts and get the blood moving again throughout the Marriott enterprise." Bollenbach's plan was controversial and some of the company's bondholders attacked it, but it was no financial "bait and switch" tactic. "In the aggressive atmosphere of the 1980s, we had let ourselves get pulled too far away from what we really were," explained Marriott. "Steve's plan would get us back to our core identity: Marriott was (and is) not about debt, real estate ownership, and deals; we're about *management and service*." The plan worked and within three years, the stocks of both companies had risen 185 percent.

Bollenbach became the CEO of Host Marriott and went on to become CFO of The Walt Disney Company, where he was instrumental in the $19 billion acquisition of Capital Cities/ABC. In 1996, he was named President and CEO of Hilton Hotels Corporation. In 1997, when he launched a $6.5 billion bid for ITT, *Fortune* reported "if you had invested $1 in Bollenbach's employers beginning in 1982 and moved your money each time he switched jobs, you would have $38.76 today, an annual growth rate of almost 28%." That is the catalytic power that financial acuity can have on careers and companies.

Former Chairman and CEO of Honeywell International Larry Bossidy and consultant Ram Charan would likely identify Bollenbach's financial skill as "business savvy," a leadership quality that they say has "become absolutely indispensable today." What is business savvy? They explain:

> People often use the phrase [*business savvy*] to describe really astute business leaders, the kind of people who possess a shrewd, instinctual feel about how to make money. Business savvy distinguishes those who over time consistently make their businesses succeed from those who have the occasional stroke of genius or lucky break.

There is another very good reason why the first and most important FISO Factor catalyst is financial acuity. Today, corporate leaders are legally obligated to stand behind the numbers that their companies report. A mastery of finance can be an important tool for a manager to use in developing this shrewd, instinctual feel. Business instinct comes from understanding and experience—it is not innate. A firm grounding in finance provides the understanding necessary to make reasonable projections and extrapolations from present business conditions.

In the wake of the ethical lapses and outright frauds of recent years, new legislation, such as the Sarbanes-Oxley Act, and judicial decisions are extending the limits of corporate liability to include senior corporate officials, such as CFOs, CEOs, and boards of directors. "I'm not an accountant," the excuse that Enron's CEO Jeffery Skilling repeatedly offered the Senate committee investigating the financial manipulations that led to his company's bankruptcy, is no longer a viable defense. Today, if you do not understand your company's financial reports, you may be placing yourself in personal jeopardy.

Of course, financial acuity does not require that you demonstrate the genius of a Steve Bollenbach. But, if you aspire to lead in today's business world you must have and know how to utilize this catalyst. Having a sense of curiosity will often lead you to dig further and further allowing you to develop financial acumen until you are comfortable with the discoveries you made.

Financial acuity yields confidence. It enables aspiring leaders to speak the common language of business, an important component of fitting in. Just as important, it provides a platform for effective and creative decision making. The insights derived through financial acuity enable aspiring leaders to position their companies' resources for greater returns, and thus, stand out.

Integrity

Financial acuity is tempered and guided by the second FISO Factor catalyst, integrity. Integrity is honesty in action. Leadership without integrity results in dishonesty and corruption.

Historically, the integrity of corporate leaders has often been questioned. The Robber Barons of the late 19th century, men such as Andrew Carnegie, John D. Rockefeller, Cornelius and William Vanderbilt, and J. P. Morgan, were accused of building great personal fortunes by unsavory means. Interestingly, the widespread use of the derogatory label dates to the 1930s and the era of the Great Depression, which is often blamed on the manipulations of business leaders or poor government responses. During both world wars, corporate leaders were accused of profiteering.

The public view of integrity in business has not improved markedly in the past quarter century. The looting of the savings and loan industry and the collapse of Michael Miliken's junk bond empire confirmed many observers' worst opinions of business. The rash of scandals that erupted in the wake of 2001's market collapse exacerbated the crisis in trust.

Justified or not, with each lapse in integrity, the public demands a higher standard for corporate and leadership integrity. Corporations and their leaders must struggle against prevailing opinion to create trust, climbing upward step-by-step. Conversely, this trust, hard-won from stakeholders, the public, and the media, can be totally lost with a single ethical lapse, real or perceived.

In late 2004, highly regarded pharmaceutical giant Merck & Company, Inc., and its CEO Raymond Gilmartin ran headlong into the integrity buzz saw. On September 30, Merck voluntarily withdrew its best-selling arthritis drug Vioxx from the market. It announced that a company-sponsored study had discovered that long-term use of the drug, which brought the company $2.5 billion in revenue in 2003, raised the risk of heart attack and stroke to unacceptable levels.

This seemed a responsible and ethical reaction on the part of the company. "We are taking this action because we believe it best serves the interests of patients," explained Gilmartin. "Although we believe it would have been possible to continue to market Vioxx with labeling that would incorporate this new data, given the ability of alternative therapies, and the questions raised by the data, we concluded that a voluntary withdrawal is the responsible course to take."

Within days, however, dissenting opinions began to appear. It was claimed that Merck had been slow to respond to and ignored the results of earlier studies that suggested that Vioxx had dangerous cardiovascular side effects. Merck's leader responded logically, explaining why the company believed that these studies had not been definitive. Gilmartin reiterated that the company had acted responsibly, but the controversy continued to grow. Both Merck and the Food and Drug Administration were attacked. The Justice Department opened an investigation; the Securities and Exchange Commission announced an informal inquiry.

By mid-November, Merck stock had dropped from its preannouncement level of $47 to $27 and three credit-rating firms cut Merck's debt rating, thus considerably increasing its interest expense and tarnishing its future ability to borrow. By that time, over 400 Vioxx-related lawsuits had been filed against the company and there were calls for Gilmartin's resignation. It remains to be seen if Merck and Gilmartin have actually acted improperly, but it is already clear that the catalytic power of integrity has worked against the company.

The second catalytic agent of the FISO Factor is integrity because without it, you cannot discern the lines between appropriate and inappropriate behavior. Integrity is the litmus test by which organizational and personal actions are guided and measured.

Integrity yields trust. When aspiring leaders play by the rules and act consistently with ethical values, they fit in. They are seen as trusted members of their organizations. When aspiring leaders maintain the rules, that is, stand by established ethical standards and blow the whistle to stop play when those standards are breached, they stand out. They demonstrate the courage of their convictions and live up to the trust they have earned.

Linkages

The emergence of the Internet made everyone aware of the new speed of information and how interconnected we are. The fact is we live and work in a networked world. It is the linkages between ideas, people, and actions that connect networks and give them form and substance.

Leaders must be expert at creating linkages and forming them into networks. This third catalyst of the FISO Factor is not aimed at the card-exchanging, glad-handing networking for personal gain that drives multilevel marketing schemes and that aggressive salespeople are urged to practice. Rather, it is an important component of a leader's work. Linkages are the means by which strategies are converted into action.

When Accenture Fellow and Babson College professor Tom Davenport, University of Virginia professor Rob Cross, and Accenture research fellow Susan Cantrell studied knowledge workers (middle managers and other professionals) in four different organizations, they found that linkages play a critical role in performance. They reported:

> What really distinguishes high performers from the rest of the pack is their ability to maintain and leverage personal networks. The most effective knowledge workers create and tap large, diversified networks that are rich in experience and span all organizational boundaries.

Michael Eisner, the CEO of the Walt Disney Company, illustrates both the positive and negative power that is inherent in the catalyst of linkages. In 1984, when Eisner, along with the late Frank Wells, picked up the leadership reins at Disney, that company was moribund. Since the deaths of Walt and Roy O. Disney, the company founders, the management had held firmly to its focus on family entertainment, but it had lost the creative spark that made Disney an integral part of American family life.

Eisner revitalized Disney with a host of new creative linkages. He forged a productive working relationship with Roy E. Disney, Walt's nephew and company cofounder Roy O. Disney's son. He linked up with Jeffrey Katzenbach and rebuilt the Disney film studio, forming creative alliances with Steve Jobs's Pixar Animation Studios and with Harvey and Bob Weinstein at Miramax, which Disney acquired. He engaged world-class architects, such as Michael Graves and Robert A.M. Stern, to build the Disney vision of entertainment into the very structure of the company's theme parks, hotels, and headquarters.

All of these creative linkages and more drove Disney's results through the end of the century. In 1999, the company's annual revenues approached $24 billion. Disney stockholders had realized a 24 percent compound annual return over the 15 years since Eisner had taken on the leadership of their company.

In recent years, however, Eisner's ability to maintain effective linkages has faltered and so have the company's earnings. Roy Disney, who accused Eisner of creating a "brain drain" and resigned from the company and its board, announced that 2004 earnings would only "approximate those achieved seven years ago." After long negotiation, Steve Jobs decided that Pixar would not renew its partnership with Disney in 2005. The Weinsteins are also reportedly unhappy in their relationship with Eisner and Disney.

In March 2004, Roy Disney led a very public revolt against Eisner that resulted in 45 percent of shareholders voting against management's slate of directors, which included Eisner himself. In September 2004, Eisner announced he would leave Disney when his contract is complete in 2006. In a very real sense, the same catalyst that drove his success has also powered his descent. Events accelerated after Eisner articulated his departure plan. On March 13, 2005, The Walt Disney Company announced that the Board of Directors had unanimously elected a new chief executive officer, Robert Iger, to assume the position of CEO on October 1, 2005. Both Iger and Eisner will share chief executive duties over the next 6 months. Eisner said he would not seek another term on the company's board nor will he pursue the chairmanship after the current chairman retires at the company's annual meeting in 2006. Linkages are the third catalytic agent of the FISO Factor because these connections open the doors to the resources, thinking, and support needed to achieve organizational objectives. Linkages represent the support network of aspiring leaders.

Linkages yield access. They are the basis of the internal network that aspiring leaders need to fit into an organization. Linkages also generate the right information at the right time and enable the fast response that allows aspiring leaders to stand out.

Learning

"Past results are no guarantee of future returns." Every investor is familiar with that gloomy sentence; it is the part of the boilerplate that warns them that their money is at risk. Leaders also need to heed that warning because what worked in the past will not work forever. Organizations and people must learn in order to change and grow. Learning, the fourth catalytic agent of the FISO Factor, is the element that enables corporate and personal growth.

The importance of learning has risen to the forefront of the corporate consciousness in the past 15 years. More recently, after conducting a study identifying and analyzing companies that had been able to boost their performance from "good to great," management researcher and consultant Jim Collins, pegged "disciplined thought" as one of the three stages in that transformation.

One of the components of disciplined thought, according to Collins, is the ability and willingness to "confront the brutal facts." This requires a rigorous learning process that enables leaders and organizations to face up to their current reality, to surface truths wherever they might be found, and to derive lessons from failure.

What holds true for companies also holds true for leaders. How does a good leader become a great leader? "Great leaders don't give better answers; they ask better questions. And they ask them repeatedly," says Collins. "It's all about disciplined thought, understanding the challenges." It is about listening and learning, instead of telling and directing.

This energetic, almost frenetic, focus on learning was certainly characterized by Jack Welch during his tenure as CEO of General Electric Company. Welch's concept of GE as a "boundaryless organization" was based in part on his demand that the company be open to good ideas from any source. The now famous GE work-out program, instituted in 1988, supported the concept. In work-out sessions, employees were brought together to surface problems and create solutions. Managers were forced to quickly consider and immediately approve feasible proposals and the employees were turned loose to take action. By mid-1993, over 200,000 GEers had participated in work-outs and 80 percent of the proposals they generated had been approved. In a 1994 interview, Welch explained:

> Productivity is the belief that there's an infinite capacity to improve anything. We live here *knowing* we don't have the answers. We know *somebody* has the answers. We're out there chasing every day to find them, because it's intellectual capital that creates productivity.
>
> The quality of an idea does not depend on its altitude in the organization. An idea will come from any source. So we will search the globe for ideas. We will share what we know with others to get what they know. We have a constant quest to raise the bar, and we get there by constantly talking to others.

Learning yields innovation. It is through the process of gathering and synthesizing data that aspiring leaders understand and fit into the culture and processes at work within their organizations. It is also an important key to standing out—all progress, whether it is incremental or breakthrough, is created through the FISO Factor catalyst of learning.

Perspective

Diversity, which can be generally defined as recognizing, embracing, and valuing the differences between people, has become a major issue in the corporate world. Why is diversity of such importance to business? The answer, in a word, is *perspective*, the fifth catalytic agent of the FISO Factor.

Perspective is critical to a leader's decision-making process. Leaders must seek out alternative points of view in order to learn, reach sound decisions, and effectively communicate with and influence the various constituencies connected with their businesses.

The process of gathering perspectives often produces surprises. Take the famous Johnson & Johnson Tylenol poisoning case from 1982. J&J's reaction to the criminal tampering with its best-selling product is still cited as a classic case of corporate crisis response and integrity, but it also offers an interesting lesson in the need to gather a full spectrum of views.

J&J's senior management quickly reached the decision to remove every Tylenol capsule from circulation, a nationwide task that included asking consumers to dispose of any Tylenol capsules in their possession and replacing them with tamper-proof Tylenol tablets at the company's expense. But, when J&J informed the FDA and FBI of this landmark decision, both agencies initially opposed it! They argued that the recall would represent a capitulation to the terrorist who had poisoned the capsules and encourage copycat crimes.

This new perspective gave J&J pause, but the company decided to go ahead with the recall. Chairman James Burke said, "Someone was using our brand as a vehicle for murder, and we had to remove the vehicle." In this case, it was the right response and lives were saved when two more bottles with poisoned capsules were recovered.

The more powerful the leader, the more important alternative perspectives become. I introduced Michael Maccoby and his concept of "productive narcissists" in the last chapter. Maccoby says that these superleaders tend to be highly independent and often isolate themselves from others. As a result, their decisions can become fatally flawed.

How can they overcome this dangerous habit? "Find a trusted side-kick," advises Maccoby. He reports that a close and trusted colleague offers a leader the additional perspective that they often need in order to properly evaluate ideas and surface flawed thinking. In the case of Disney's Michael Eisner, a fine example of a high-achieving productive narcissist, many observers think that Frank Wells provided this kind of service and perspective to him. It was only after Wells was tragically killed in a helicopter crash that the linkages that enabled Disney's success began to deteriorate.

Perspective yields balanced judgment. Effective leaders see the big picture by understanding and addressing the concerns of their constituent groups before they formulate their action plans. They learn to fit in by identifying the many internal perspectives present within their organizations. They stand out by reaching out for external perspectives and bringing new viewpoints into the organization.

Global Citizenship

Fifty years ago, international business was a specialized topic, mainly of interest in a handful of giant corporations. Since then, the purview of large, midsize, and many small businesses has inexorably expanded from the national level to the global level. The final catalytic agent of the FISO Factor is global citizenship because the world of business has transcended national boundaries. Corporate performance and career success are now dependent on the ability to operate across borders and embrace the diversity of the world's peoples and cultures.

The catalytic mindset in global business can be found in the difference between the words *emigrant* and *immigrant*. Many leaders and their companies approach global markets with the mindset of an emigrant. They are focused on where they are *coming from* and how they will implant their ways on the world. They think of themselves as colonists. This is a natural instinct; humans tend to see the world from the inside out. As history proves, however, colonialism is usually a prescription for failure.

Instead, aspiring leaders need to approach the world with the mindset of an immigrant. They must focus on where they are *going* and view the world from the outside in. They see themselves as citizens of their new home countries. They think about what they can learn and how they will fit in and provide value in these new markets.

INSEAD professors Yves Doz, José Santos, and Peter Williamson call companies and leaders who can successfully adopt the immigrant mindset "metanationals." Metanationals operate at a level above global leaders and companies. They describe the work of becoming metanational in terms of a race:

> It is about winning a global tournament played at three different levels: It is a race to identify and access new technologies and market trends ahead of the competition, a race to turn this dispersed knowledge into innovative products and services, and a race to scale and exploit these innovations in markets around the world.

Société BIC, the company that made the disposable ballpoint pen a global product, is a good example of a company that was built on the catalyst of global citizenship. Just ask a half dozen people where BIC is headquartered; most will not know the right answer. BIC is a French company headquartered in Paris. Today, it is led by Bruno Bich, the son of company founder Marcel Bich.

The French are often accused of national parochialism, but the BIC story does not support that view. Marcel Bich actually discovered the ballpoint pen in England in the years following World War II. He immediately recognized its advantages over the fountain pen, purchased the rights to it, refined it, and in 1950, introduced the BIC pen to Europe. Marcel was a great traveler and within just a few years, he created a global network of distribution partners for his pens. In 1956, he launched operations in Brazil. By 1958, he entered the U.S., Middle East, and Africa markets. In 1965, he entered the Japanese market.

BIC's current leader, Bruno Bich, is just as much a global citizen as his father. Bruno was educated in the United States and led BIC's U.S. operations after his schooling. Bruno built BIC's presence in the United States until its pens were a ubiquitous feature of the culture. He did it by acting as an immigrant: BIC's marketing and sales efforts in the United States were designed for U.S. consumers and management transferred production to the United States and changed products when economically feasible. Creating the best product attributes from the United States and from France optimized the customer offering.

Today, BIC is the world's leading maker of ballpoint pens and a leader in three product areas: stationery, lighters, and shavers. Over 22 million BIC pens, 4 million BIC lighters, and 11 million BIC shavers are purchased worldwide, each day.

Global citizenship yields agility. It means living a life in business that recognizes the worldwide implications of your acts. In the growing awareness of the values, priorities, and limitations of other cultures, and in the acknowledgment of the interdependencies between nations, aspiring leaders fit into the broader world of business. In exploring the rich diversity that characterizes our world, aspiring leaders stand out for their ability to tap into valuable sources of ideas and innovations.

THE FISO FACTOR CATALYSTS AND YOUR LEADERSHIP PLATFORM

The six catalytic agents of the FISO Factor—financial acuity, integrity, linkages, learning, perspective, and global citizenship—combine to

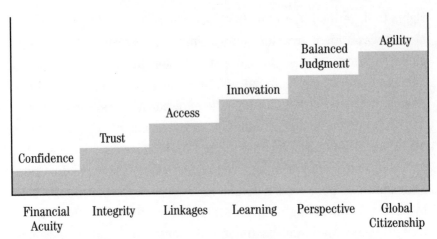

Figure 3-1   The Six Catalysts of the FISO Factor and Their Yields

create a powerful platform for leadership. Together, the six agents lead to a higher level of effective and successful leadership, and ultimately, to the C-suite. As Figure 3-1 indicates, some of the agents are more integrative in nature and others are more transformative.

One by one, these agents build upon one another. Each of the catalysts contributes important support to the imperatives of fitting-in and standing-out. But they can be varied in their emphasis and effect. For instance, aspiring leaders in new positions should be focused on the power to help them fit in. Those leaders who are already established should be thinking in terms of standing-out.

Further, I recommend that you develop the catalytic agents in the order in which they have been presented. Think of the first three catalysts—financial acuity, integrity, and linkages—as the antes in today's leadership game. They provide the confidence, trust, and access you will need to take a place at the table. You cannot reach the higher levels of leadership until you master them and they enable you to demonstrate your ability to fit in. The second three catalysts—learning, perspective, and global citizenship—allow you to raise your bets. They provide the innovative ideas, balanced judgment, and agility that you will need to advance to the peak of your profession. They enable you to supercharge your leadership potential.

Picture the catalysts as a stack of six platforms. As you construct each platform, you are building the solid foundation needed to reach the next level of FISO Factor leadership.

FINANCIAL ACUITY:
THE LANGUAGE OF BUSINESS

E very profession has a specialized language. That language is a reflection of the profession's purpose, its processes, and most important, its goals. Medical doctors speak a physiological language. Architects speak a language of design and engineering. In business, we speak the language of finance.

The language of business is often mistakenly characterized as a solely numerical one. Indeed, it sometimes seems as if we do talk endlessly about "the numbers." However, as in any quantitative dialect, numbers are merely representations of ideas. The numbers represent corporate goals, performances, and results. The intent of business is to create wealth through added value. The language of finance gives expression to that intent.

Pamela Forbes Lieberman is a leader who understands the numbers. In November 2001, Pamela was tapped to serve as the CEO of the

TruServ Corporation (now True Value Company). TruServ is a $2 billion wholesale hardware co-op, which serves 6,100 independently owned stores operating under True Value, Taylor Rental, Party Central, and several other brand names.

In 1997, in an effort to remain competitive in the face of growing competition from big-box home improvement chains, such as Lowe's and Home Depot, ServiStar/Coast to Coast merged with Cotter & Company to form TruServ. Unfortunately, the merger proved difficult and debt rose precipitously. In 1999, the co-op announced a loss of $130.8 million. The value of the dealer-member stock dropped by 65 percent and the company declared a moratorium on stock redemptions. In 2000, sales dropped by $500 million, and a $23 million loss was declared. In 2001, when Pamela was hired with a mandate to restructure the company's finances, TruServ faced default on covenants involving $200 million in debt and needed to renegotiate terms of its debt with lenders or else declare bankruptcy.

When Pamela was appointed CEO (one of only 11 women CEOs in the Fortune 1000), one TruServ dealer-member emailed another, "What does she know about plumbing?" The return message said, "I don't think we have a plumbing problem."

What Pamela does know is business finance. She created a five-member team that examined the company's situation and established a ten-point plan designed to return TruServ to profitability. She reduced inventory and closed underutilized distribution centers, sold off manufacturing operations that diffused the company's focus, and cut administrative staff levels. These actions, and others, strengthened the company's balance sheet, reduced operating costs, and increased margins. Within a year, the company was stable and profitable once more. In 2003, this demonstration of financial acuity convinced lenders to provide a $275 million credit line that enabled TruServ to refinance its debt and cut interest expenses by more than 50 percent. By November 2004, when Pamela left TruServ, the restructuring was complete, the moratorium on stock redemptions finally lifted, and the company was preparing to move into a new phase of growth. Like Pamela, the most successful leaders are those that best understand the connection between numbers and fulfilling business intentions. They have financial acuity—a perceptive keenness that enables them to identify and manage those activities and assets that will create the greatest positive influence on the numbers. Financial acuity is the ability to understand, use, and communicate the underlying principles and implications of financial statements and the broader economic trends to best position your company's resources for profitable returns.

CRACKING THE CORPORATE CODE

Each of the six catalytic agents in the FISO Factor introduced in Chapter 3 can be shown on a spectrum. One end of the spectrum is fitting-in; the other is standing-out. When we plot the spectrum for financial acuity, as shown in Figure 4-1, we find that its most powerful influence can be realized near the "fitting-in" end of the spectrum. In other words, the primary power of the financial acuity catalyst is its ability to help aspiring leaders fit in.

Let's return to Pamela Lieberman and TruServ for a moment. It is clear that Pamela used her financial acuity to stand out at TruServ, but more impressively, she also used it to quickly and effectively fit in. She was first hired as the company's CFO in March 2001. Four months later, after the COO resigned, she was appointed to that job in addition to her responsibilities as CFO. Four months after that, she was named CEO. In eight months, and in the middle of a highly chaotic environment, this outsider in terms of industry experience, corporate culture, and gender established herself as the right person for the job each time a new opportunity appeared. With the help of financial acuity, Pamela cracked the corporate code at TruServ.

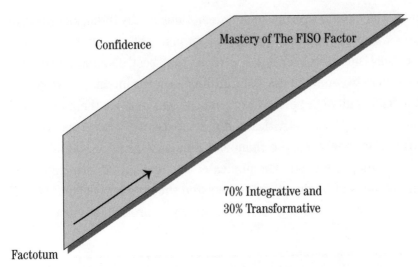

Figure 4-1   The Catalytic Spectrum for Financial Acuity

The reason for this is that the goals of the corporation, to create wealth through added value, required, at that time, more reliance upon financial expertise than upon industry knowledge. The board, management, and other employees all realized or bought into this need. Pamela "fit" the needs of the company because the company needed financial expertise. But, one might argue, the TruServ example is an extreme case—not appropriate to prove a general rule. It is not as unusual or extreme as one might suppose. All businesses, regardless of industry, rely upon financial decision makers. Finance is the common language among disparate businesses that differ by industry, style, organizational form, and market. Strong financial acuity guarantees fitting in" to some extent—wherever one might be working.

Conversely, a dearth of financial acuity can just as quickly sabotage your future at a company. The story of John Walter and AT&T Corporation provides a graphic example. Walter was hired by AT&T as president and COO in 1996. The ex-CEO of printer R.R. Donnelley & Sons Co. was supposed to serve in that capacity until January 1998, when he would replace Robert Allen as AT&T's CEO. But Walter never demonstrated the financial acuity needed to fit in at AT&T.

According to Dick Martin, an AT&T public relations executive during that period, CEO Allen heard "complaints about Walter from a steady stream of executives. . . . They said he still didn't have a grasp of the business's fundamentals and didn't seem to be making any effort to learn them." Martin continues:

> Allen himself was beginning to believe Walter was a brilliant salesman but superficial, dealing in tired bromides. At one board meeting just before the executive session when Allen met alone with the outside members, Allen asked Walter to give an operational review. He spent twenty minutes talking about his efforts to instill a sense of ownership into the company's employees, told [a favorite Ross Perot] story, and ended by declaring that AT&T had all the elements to be a winning, learning organization. When he left the room, Allen simply said, "See what I mean?"

In July 1997, AT&T's board announced that Walter was not ready to assume the CEO post by year end. Walter was compelled to resign; AT&T paid out over $25 million for less than a year of his time. It was a lose-lose situation for the company's management succession plans and the shareholders. John Walter was publicly dismissed.

How can you avoid false starts and develop the financial acuity needed to crack the code to success? Building your fluency in the language of finance is a three-step process: learn the basics, identify your financial focus, and frame your work.

Learn the Basics

You were not born speaking the language of finance and, unless your parents are accountants, you probably did not pick it up at the dinner table. So it is altogether understandable if you do not speak the language . . . yet. In fact, most businesspeople don't.

There is good reason for this: Managers and executives are often intently focused on other areas. Société BIC, for instance, was historically focused on operational concerns, that is, producing and selling great products at the lowest possible cost. As a result, there was a widespread lack of financial fluency within the company. As CFO, I was dismayed to discover that 18 of 21 country managers from around the globe did not understand the importance of DSO (days sales outstanding) on receivables. This metric, which tells you how many days elapse between when you invoice customers and when they pay, affects cash flow, the life blood of every company.

When I joined BIC, the veins through which the company's cash circulated were severely constricted. Unsurprisingly, as we tracked back to the causes of this problem, we found that DSO was high. In fact, we were often paying taxes and other payables associated with the creation and sale of goods long before we received payment from our customers. Because we were managing cash flow poorly, we had to borrow money to make these payments. This, of course, added to costs and lowered profits.

We attacked this problem by creating a "finance for nonfinance executives" training course. Once the general managers learned how to understand and track the trend of the monthly DSO along with inventory turnover metrics, we began collecting cash more quickly in many countries. This strengthened our balance sheet and improved our financial liquidity. Moreover, country managers realized real advantages in using financial understandings as a means of meeting their goals. A financial expert "fits in" very well once she is able to help managers achieve their yearly bonuses. Finance suddenly seems less foreign or less of an antagonist when other managers see how they benefit in tangible ways.

The fact that there is a widespread lack of knowledge about the basics of business finance creates a tremendous opportunity for you to stand out at the same time that you fit in, by helping the organization and those in it achieve their goals. So, if you are not already fluent in the language of finance, the way to capitalize on that opportunity is to educate yourself as quickly as possible.

Sign up for a basic business economics course designed for nonfinancial managers. Many companies offer this training internally. If your company does not, these courses are almost always available as part of the continuing education curriculum at colleges and universities. There are also many distance-learning options available. If your company offers a tuition reimbursement plan, your only investment will be your time.

Read! (This is perhaps the best and simplest piece of learning advice most of us ever hear.) There are a host of books on business finance and economics written for nonfinancial managers. Read business cases, too. And as you read the cases, observe the role that the numbers play—ways in which they are used to identify and analyze problems and opportunities, and how the actions taken positively or negatively affect them.

Identify Your Financial Focus

Once you understand the basics of the language of finance, you need to customize it for your particular situation. You accomplish this by filtering your basic knowledge of finance through two lenses. The first lens is your company. The second lens is your career. These two lenses enable you to identify your financial focus.

Your first task is to filter your financial knowledge through the company lens. Because each company is unique, it is usually pursuing specific strategies or combinations of strategies. A strategy is a time-sensitive attempt to maximize wealth through deployment of human and capital resources. This strategy may be mergers and acquisitions or innovation or six sigma or BPM (business performance management) or SCM (supply chain management) or any number of other initiatives. As often happens, your company may be simultaneously undertaking a combination of strategies.

It should not take much effort to identify your company's strategies. Ask yourself what priorities your CEO is expressing internally and externally. What are her emails about? What does his message in the annual report say about next year's corporate goals? What is the main topic in the corporate newsletter?

When you have identified your company's primary strategies, link them to the balance sheet and you will see the corporate financial focus. For instance, if the strategy is new product innovation, your company's financial focus is revenue growth. If the strategy is six sigma, the financial focus is lower COGS (cost of goods sold).

By the way, a company's financial focus will change over time, so you must remain aware that this year's answers might not be applicable next year. For example, when Pamela Lieberman joined TruServ, cutting costs and stabilizing the company's financial balance was its primary focus. As Pamela accomplished this goal, the company's financial focus began to change. At some point as the restructuring process neared completion, TruServ's focus began to shift to top-line growth. The company's next CEO has to have additional catalytic agents to produce that type of result.

The next task is to filter your finance knowledge through the lens of your career. Determine how your job is connected to the company's financial statements and its financial focus. The objective of this filtering process is to determine and create alignment between the financial goals of the company and your work activities.

This is simple logic, but misalignments between the corporate and career lenses are a very common problem. When I worked at Sara Lee Corporation as chief administrative officer, Pacific Rim, one of my responsibilities was executive staffing. On one occasion, I participated in the search for a new general manager in our Chilean hosiery business. We had acquired this business and wanted to grow it. We hired an executive with regional and industry experience who had a well-earned reputation as a cost-cutter. This gave me pause, and in hindsight, I wish I had been more vocal about my misgivings. Contrary to the corporate focus, the new GM did everything he could to reduce costs and very little to increase revenue. Worse, the pressure of the relentless cost reduction caused a workforce revolt. The union declared a strike and, of course, revenues fell off a cliff. The business never did recover. We ended up winding down the operation instead of growing it.

The career lesson here: Be acutely aware of how your performance is aligned to corporate goals. When you align the view seen through the corporate lens with the view seen through the career lens, you have created a financial focus that will lead to leadership success.

Frame Your Work

Once you comprehend the basics of finance and can relate them to your company and career, it is time to begin speaking the language of finance. The final step in the mindset shift required for financial acuity is the framing of your ideas and your activities, and how you communicate them, around your financial focus.

For decades, many business leaders seemed to have an almost genetic disdain for employee ideas. Before selling Eastern Airlines out from under its employees to raider Frank Lorenzo in 1986, CEO Frank Borman infamously summarized this view, saying, "I'm not going to have the monkeys running the zoo." This is, of course, a severely flawed perspective (Lorenzo, who also had a low opinion of employee involvement, flew Eastern into bankruptcy), but its roots reach down to one hard truth: Many employees often fail to analyze and present their ideas effectively.

The truth is too many of us are *functionally limited* in our ability to create sound ideas and communicate their value. In other words, our mindset and our messages are limited by the boundaries of our jobs. Sometimes, this is caused by functional tunnel vision. For instance, the ideas of a manufacturing manager, who thinks only of increasing capacity and production output in the midst of a recession in which finished inventory is piling up, are sure to fall on unsympathetic ears. At other times, it is a matter of presentation. A good idea that is explained poorly—that is not connected to the greater needs of the company—will often be misunderstood and treated as a bad idea.

The solutions to these problems are simple. First, we need to ensure that our work and ideas connect to the financial needs of the company. Second, we need to articulate that connection at every opportunity. We need to frame our messages in a way that will enable others to understand them.

A good way to accomplish this is to establish the connections before you begin presenting ideas. For instance, whenever I begin a new job, I create a list of objectives that are based on the financial focus of the position. I recognize, however, that these objectives are based on assumptions that may or may not be correct. So, before I set to work, I always request a meeting with my boss to confirm that my objectives are sound. (See the accompanying examples from my tenure at Société BIC.) This process not only refines my plan; it ensures that I spend my time as effectively as possible.

OBJECTIVES AT SOCIÉTÉ BIC

This is the preliminary list of objectives I created during my first month as CFO at BIC:

- Build long-term financial strength of the company
- Establish AA credit rating
- Grow base business and make qualified acquisitions
- Hire and retain world-class people

- Improve ROE (return on earnings) to improve shareholder value
- Improve financial management
- Participate in dynamic growth in digital economy
- Streamline financial reporting
- Better analyze and manage risks
- Implement analysis disciplines for capital investments and/or acquisitions
- Review balance sheet to create shareholder value

REFINED OBJECTIVES AT SOCIÉTÉ BIC

This is the refined, prioritized, and confirmed list of objectives that emerged after my meeting with CEO Bruno Bich:

- Know where we are: where profits derived
- Higher risks, need more safety net
- Determine resource allocation and comparisons
  - To expectation (last year and budget)
  - To other divisions
  - To the competitive set
- Maintain visibility of KPI benchmarks [BIC had previously established seven key performance indicators]
- Analyze and make appropriate acquisitions as needed to build shareholder value
- Ensure Investor Relations communicates transparency of existing business and direction in future.

In the BIC example, after arming myself with this financial focus and the support of my boss, I was ready to begin to make decisions and take action.

Now, of course, I was a CFO at BIC. Finding connections between my job and the financial needs of the company did not pose a substantial problem. But, what if one is a marketing manager? In such a case, the marketing programs and recommendations still must be rooted to the financial objectives. Otherwise, they will be merely ideas blowing in the wind without the proper rationale for long-term support.

THE HABITS OF FINANCIALLY ACUTE LEADERS

As you gain experience and get comfortable using the catalyst of financial acuity, you can begin to hone your new talent. Leaders who are masters of this catalyst exhibit several common behaviors: Masters of financial acuity relentlessly dig into the numbers; they act on the financial knowledge they collect; and, they do everything in their power to encourage others to master this catalyst too.

Dig into the Numbers

Watching Microsoft CEO Steve Ballmer, a fellow director at consulting giant Accenture Ltd, tear into the numbers is an energizing experience. Whether we are discussing new initiatives or compensation plans, Steve is always trying to ferret out the costs and he will not desist until he understands the bottom line.

For instance, Accenture is in the process of a shift in the balance between its core business of consulting to its outsourcing business. Steve is not content to discuss the percentages of this shift (the overall ratio of outsourcing to consulting). He instinctively digs down to understand the margins. This is a critical issue: Outsourcing is a lower margin business than consulting, so any shift to outsourcing will have a proportionate adverse effect on the firm's margins. Steve wants to know what that effect will be now and in the future on Accenture's financial results. More importantly, he wants to know management's plan for maintaining the margins.

You can also see Steve's predilection for digging into the numbers in his actions at Microsoft. He argued aggressively and successfully to convince Bill Gates to reorganize the software giant into seven operating divisions with their own profit and loss statements. The result was that the company's management was able to improve its understanding of where and how Microsoft made money. "The numbers," further reported *Fortune*, "laid bare to the world money-losing operations like the MSN online service, the Xbox game machine, and software for cell phones and PDAs."

Digging into the numbers is not just an intellectual exercise; it is also a physical one. You must also act like a detective and dig into the source of the numbers. At Sara Lee, I was sent to Finland to perform due diligence during the acquisition of a Finnish hosiery and knitwear company. Inside one of the company's warehouses, I found large quantities of finished goods prepared specifically for export to Russia, a country that was undergoing tremendous economic upheaval at the time. I was also told that there was no reason to be concerned because the Finnish government guaranteed receivables on goods sent to Russia as part of its trade policy. However, several evenings later, at dinner with a senior executive, I learned that the trade policy was being eliminated. Those goods, I realized, might never be sold and were not valued properly in the acquisition.

Act on Your Findings

No matter how keen your understanding of the numbers, it matter's little if you do not act on your knowledge. The letter of intent and the terms of Sara Lee's purchase of the Finnish hosiery and knitwear company were already in place when I discovered the unsold Russian inventory. Further, it was not a comfortable job reporting back to Sara Lee's senior management team that the proposed deal was flawed. Nevertheless, I did and the entire acquisition was renegotiated.

The corporate world is very focused on financial reporting these days. In addition to the new legal requirements of Sarbanes-Oxley, corporate leaders realize that they must have the performance metrics and real-time financial results at their fingertips. But data generation is not an end in and of itself, it is meant to enable business leaders to act with confidence.

In 1998, while I served as CFO of Scarborough, Maine-based Hannaford Bros. Co. (now owned by the Delhaize Group), the company implemented a multi-million-dollar information system that tracked inventory as it was sold. This was a vast improvement over the way the typical supermarket tracked inventory at the time, and it enabled us to always know exactly what was on our stores' shelves and how fast the inventory was moving off the shelves.

Why was this information valuable? It allowed us to quickly act in concert with customer demand. We increased inventory turns from 12 to 12.6 and reduced DWC (days working capital) from 8 to 6.9 at a time at which the industry norm was 21.6 DWC. Further, Hannaford's profit margins after taxes grew to 3.2 percent, well above the industry average of 2 percent. When Delhaize acquired the company, it paid the highest P-E multiple in the industry. We achieved these results not because we captured the data, but because we acted on it.

Foster Financial Acuity Companywide

It is tempting to think of financial acuity as a personal weapon for enhancing your leadership career, but if you act on that temptation you will never capture its full catalytic power. The full potential of financial acuity is released when you foster its use throughout your department or division or company. When everyone who reports to you possesses financial acuity, your organization's results will truly become supercharged.

Proven results are the reason why so many companies are pursuing financial literacy for the entire workforce. The story of Avon, OH-based Manco, Inc. is an excellent case in point. In 1971, Jack Kahl purchased Manco, a small industrial tape manufacturer with annual revenues of $800,000, for $192,000. Kahl went on to create the Duck Tape brand and over three decades, through innovative, consumer-friendly packaging and creative sales and marketing, built the brand into the nation's best-selling duct tape with over 60 percent of the market.

One of the most positively noted features at Manco during Kahl's tenure was the fact that throughout the company, the entire financial picture was prominently featured for all to see. Duct tape–lined charts traced three years of sales results. Daily sales were charted on chalkboards, as well as shipments, invoicing, expenses, and monthly profit and loss figures. Bar charts plotted the value of the stock in the employee stock ownership plan. News, such as important new sales accounts, was transmitted on LED displays. Kahl also made a practice of reviewing the monthly P&L in a companywide meeting.

To further focus employee attention on financial goals, Kahl would pose competitive challenges. In 1990, in the cold Ohio winter, he swam the pond at company headquarters after the company hit its sales target. In 1997, he shaved his head. In 1999, he spent several hundred thousand dollars of his own money to rent a Cleveland theater and import several Broadway stars to entertain the entire workforce for an evening. (Of course, it helped to have hired employees who actually took an interest in such eccentric behavior—it would not work everywhere.)

Kahl's emphasis on financial acuity paid off. In the late 1990s, Germany's Henkel Group acquired Manco for $116 million. In 2000, when Kahl retired and his son John took over as CEO, the company's annual revenues were approaching $300 million.

Manco's larger brethren are also aware of the catalytic power of financial acuity. At Dallas, TX-based Verizon Information Services, the publishing arm of telecom giant Verizon, management wants to ensure that employees know how their jobs connect to the corporate business strategy. To foster that understanding, employees are trained in the basics of business finance and then, they are turned loose to apply that knowledge in simulation games that put them in charge of multi-million-dollar companies. "I want all employees to think like they are owners of the business," says executive director of workforce performance Julie Bollinger. Indeed, that is the best reason for encouraging the development of financial acuity.

FINANCIAL ACUITY YIELDS CONFIDENCE

Knowledge creates confidence; and this is certainly true regarding business finance. The ultimate payoff for developing your financial acuity is *confidence*. When you can conduct a fact-based analysis, tie it to the financial goals of the company, and reach a sound, well-supported decision, you can recommend a course of action with confidence. Further, although there is uncertainty and risk in every decision, your batting average is sure to rise, as is your reputation as a leader.

Like Bob Lipp, the chairman of St. Paul Travelers, you will be able to effectively focus your attention. As a director on the company's board, I watch Bob quickly and confidently appraise the myriad issues we are asked to consider. He knows when to dig deeper into a situation and when to stay out of the trench. He is always thinking in terms of financial impact . . . on corporate performance and shareholder value. And he is always looking for the leverage point where he can make the largest impact.

Like Larry Bossidy, Honeywell's former chief, you will be able to reach sound decisions. Bossidy likes to tell the story of a turbogenerator business whose development he approved. Unfortunately, during the development process, the market for the product, which had already required a large investment, began to disappear. "My first intuition was to say, 'Yes, these problems are correctable," recalls Bossidy. "But when I looked at the amount of money needed to correct them vs. spending the money someplace else, I closed it down. It really wasn't a tough decision. It was an emotional decision, because I still think there's a place for this kind of turbogenerator in the economy. On the other hand, it's going to take a long time for it to happen. Given the other funding requests around the company, it didn't make the cut. One of the things you do in a . . . company is to make these kinds of choices quickly; you don't let them linger. And so, reluctantly but decisively, I decided to get out."

Finally, unlike the management team at Kraft Foods, you will be able to act in a timely manner. In 1988, while I worked at Kraft, the company decided to sell its Duracell division and received $550 million in cash at the closing of the deal. But the issue of reinvesting the money, which was one of the key budgetary considerations of that year, was not so efficiently dispatched. In fact, management could not decide what to do with the windfall and did not act. Instead, the money became a bull's-eye and, at the end of 1988, Philip Morris swooped in and acquired Kraft Foods, as well the tidy sum on its balance sheet.

Clearly, developing your financial acuity and building the confidence you need to analyze, decide, and act on the business issues in your company will enable you to fit in and stand out as a savvy business leader.

THE ABCS OF FINANCIAL ACUITY

Each of the six catalytic agents requires a certain attitude, behavior and characteristic for fitting-in as well as standing-out. Here are some thought-starter questions for financial acuity.

Fitting In with Financial Acuity

Attitude: Shift your mindset. What are the top three financial focal points in your company? How is your position connected to them?

Behavior: Sit down with your boss. What are your objectives? How can you align the lenses of company and career and better focus your approach to your job?

Characteristic: Speak the language of finance. What knowledge do you require to build your financial fluency? How can you reframe your job description to reflect your financial focus?

Standing Out with Financial Acuity

Attitude: Always be curious. What are the best-in-class benchmarks in your industry and beyond? How can you apply other peoples' ideas in your company?

Behavior: Take action. How can you transform your knowledge into creative solutions that generate revenue or cut costs? What are the simplest, least risky ways to test your ideas?

Characteristic: Make fact-based decisions. Do the numbers accurately reflect reality? How do the facts support your recommendations?

CHAPTER

5

INTEGRITY: THE LEADER'S
NORTH STAR

Integrity is the second catalytic agent of the FISO Factor. It is the catalyst that powers ethical behavior, enables consistency in thought and deed, and embraces a holistic approach to work and life. This is why integrity serves as the leader's North Star.

The North Star or Polaris has played a significant role in human history. Because it is located above the North Pole and appears to remain stationary in the night sky, the North Star has been a principal navigational beacon in the northern hemisphere for thousands of years. The ancient Phoenicians used it to crisscross the Mediterranean. In Homer's Odyssey, the goddess Calypso instructs Odysseus to keep Ursa Major, the constellation that leads us to the North Star, to his left during his epic journey home. In more recent times, Columbus used the North Star to establish the latitude during his voyages to the Americas. In the 1800s, tens of thousands of runaway African-American slaves walked toward the North Star in their harrowing journeys to freedom.

The North Star also has spiritual and mythical significance. The Navajo called it the Fire Star. They saw it as the fixed point at the center of life, the fire around which families gathered. The Skidi tribe, one of the Pawnee peoples who lived on the Great Plains, gave the North Star a particularly interesting role in their mythology. They saw how it seemed to watch over the rest of the night sky and named it the Chief Star. They believed that it was a reminder of the need for consistency and stability among tribal leaders.

Integrity is clearly the Chief Star of today's business leaders because it creates a context for everything that they do. Without integrity, leaders cannot discern the proper organizational goals and determine how to pursue them. Without integrity, they cannot properly utilize the five other catalysts of the FISO Factor and pursue career success. Neither organizations nor their leaders can survive and thrive in the long term without integrity. Consider Ivar Kreuger, the infamous Match King of the 1920s.

Kreuger was a business leader who was well endowed with all of the catalysts of the FISO Factor . . . except integrity. As odd as it sounds today, Kreuger's ambitious goal was to monopolize the worldwide market for matches. He set about accomplishing this goal by obtaining exclusive match concessions from various national governments in return for loans. He raised the money for the loans by promising investors huge returns. In fact, in the financially exuberant Roaring Twenties, Kreuger not only provided annual investment returns of 30 percent, he also obtained controlling stakes in hundreds of companies. Unfortunately, however, Kreuger's financial acuity was not complemented by integrity. He used bribes, forged bonds, outright theft, and accounting fraud to grow and maintain his empire, which crashed into bankruptcy with the onset of the Great Depression. Kreuger committed suicide in 1932.

The Match King is an extreme example of what can happen in the absence of the catalyst of integrity, but there are less dramatic examples occurring all around us everyday. In late 1999, several years before the high-profile revelations of corporate misconduct that began emerging in and after 2001, KPMG commissioned a survey of employee perceptions of organizational and leadership integrity and discovered the following disturbing statistics:

- 76 percent of employees said that they had observed violations of the law or company standards in the past 12 months.
- 61 percent of employees said that if they reported the violations to management, management would fail to discipline the responsible parties, regardless of position or rank.
- 55 percent of employees believed that their CEOs and senior executives were unapproachable if an employee needed to deliver bad news.
- 53 percent of employees said that if they reported the violations to management, management would fail to protect them from retaliation.
- 49 percent of employees said that if the misconduct they had witnessed was made public, their organizations could "significantly lose public trust."

Clearly, when three-quarters of U.S. employees are witnessing ethical and legal misconduct at work and half or more of U.S. employees believe that their leaders are not willing to address these problems, there is a crisis in integrity in the workplace. This crisis leads directly to another: Aside from the legal and financial repercussions, the crisis in integrity has created a crisis in trust.

Unsurprisingly, the crisis in trust is also well established. A CNN/USA Today/Gallup Poll in July 2002 that surveyed the American public about "people who can be trusted" found that only 23 percent believe that most CEOs of large corporations fit the bill. Almost three-quarters, 73 percent, responded that when it comes to trust, you "can't be too careful with them." To place this result in context, CEOs were ranked just above car dealers in trustworthiness. The numbers for military officers were almost exactly the reverse: 73 percent said "most can be trusted;" 24 percent said "can't be too careful with them."

How can we, as leaders, overcome odds like these and change the perceptions of the majority of our stakeholders? The answer is simple: embrace the catalytic power of integrity.

BEYOND LEGAL COMPLIANCE

You must understand integrity in all its nuances to capture its catalytic power. Too many businesspeople act as if integrity begins and ends with legal compliance. As long as they follow the letter of the law, they think that they have acted with integrity. It should go without saying that compliance to law is compulsory, but it is only the most basic component of integrity. This limited notion of integrity can help you maintain your current position (by keeping you out of jail, for one thing), but it does not have the power to create a catalytic effect on your company or your career.

British Lord Justice John Fletcher Moulton articulated the limited nature of compliance to law in a 1919 speech titled "Law and Manners." Moulton divided human action into three domains. The first was the domain of "law," in which "our actions are prescribed by laws binding upon us which must be obeyed." The next domain was "free-choice," which Moulton located at the other end of the action spectrum. It includes those actions in which there is no constraint, either external or internal, on our behavior. Finally, in between the two, said Moulton, is the domain of "manners" or ethics. This is the area of human behavior that is unenforceable by the rule of law, but in which we are not free to behave however we like. Ethics is the domain of "obedience to the unenforceable," where humans must govern their own behavior and there are no fixed legal penalties.

Much of what goes on in business falls into this domain between law and free choice. This is where integrity extends beyond legal compliance to all of those actions that may not be illegal, but nevertheless are not right.

Integrity has three facets: ethics, soundness, and completeness.

Ethics

To be an effective catalyst, integrity must be extended beyond the basic and immutable requirement of legal compliance to the concept of *ethos*—that is, the system of values defining both a leader's personal character and the character of her company. Integrity's definition has evolved over the years, but today, its primary meaning as a "steadfast adherence to strict moral or ethical code" is widely acknowledged. This means that first, a leader's ethos and the organizational ethos must be thoughtful, evident, and aligned. Second, the leader's actions must be consistent with his personal ethos and the organizational ethos. In other words, leaders with integrity seek to determine that their values and their organizations' values are ethical; then they act in accordance with those values.

Ethics is a key quality in long-term leadership success, according to leadership experts Warren Bennis and Robert Thomas. Bennis and Thomas studied lifelong leaders, those "over 70 years of age who had over a lifetime creatively responded to major changes in the organizations, markets, and/or constituencies they led." They found that their subjects "all evidenced a clear moral compass, but they didn't wear their morality on their sleeves or jam it down everyone's throat. Their behavior demonstrated that they had values, that they believed in some absolutes, and that they were guided by deep conviction."

Harvard Business School professor Donald Sull reiterated the importance of demonstrated ethical leadership when he studied corporate transformations. He found that their success was highly dependent on the ethos of their leaders. "Ethos—a leader's personal character— is crucial to building the credibility and trust necessary to persuade," says Sull. "On the other hand, a misalignment of character and commit- ment—like espousing one set of values publicly, then promoting a highly successful subordinate who blatantly flouts those values—can instantly shatter a leader's credibility." The critical need to maintain your credibility as leader leads us to the second facet of integrity.

Soundness

The second facet of integrity is "the state of being unimpaired; sound- ness." Well-constructed houses have a soundness and a solidness that you can feel when you walk their floors and close their doors. They have structural integrity. Great leaders also have this quality.

We can sense soundness in our leaders. They communicate clearly, so we know their expectations and we can trust them to act accord- ingly. This essential soundness is a quality that is often associated with highly successful leaders such as Warren Buffett. Buffett's straight-talk- ing letters in Berkshire Hathaway, Inc.'s annual reports are famous for their candor and clarity as is his consistent adherence to his highly suc- cessful investment philosophy. These reports, along with other Buffett communiqués, have often foretold the future and are always grounded in common sense, adding further luster to his reputation for soundness.

DO YOUR ACTIONS PASS THE TEST OF SOUNDNESS?

A leader's soundness is tested often and in myriad ways. I had not yet unpacked my belongings in Paris, when I was faced with just such a test. My first job as CFO was to sign off on and release BIC's semiannual earnings before the beginning of France's annual August vacation. There was just one problem: That meant the earnings had to be released within 14 days and the company's balance sheet did not balance!

As a newly hired CFO, I was in a difficult position. I could "plug" the balance sheet (artificially force it into balance) and bury the provision in a footnote, but then I would be signing off on an incomplete and perhaps, erroneous report. Further, it would directly contradict my mandate to revamp the company's financial reporting process according to international benchmarks for best practices. I could refuse to release earnings, but that would send negative signals to the investment community. Or I could "blow the whistle" and publicly report a situation that I did not yet fully understand, but that might do irreparable harm to the company.

I determined the best course by testing the soundness of alternatives. I could not sign off on an incomplete report. That would destroy my integrity and with it, my ability to make an effective case for rebuilding BIC's reporting process. It was equally wrong to go public with a situation that I had no reason to suspect hid any wrongdoing. I might well be destroying the integrity of my company for no good reason.

I opted for the middle course and told the company chairman that we had no choice but to delay the earnings report. (Happily, he agreed and I did not have to resign before my dishes were unpacked.) We minimized the fallout with investors by publicly announcing that as a new CFO, I required three months to ascertain and verify the company's financial situation. This was the reasonable and sensible solution: it gave me the time I needed to create an earnings report that was accurate *and* ensure the company's integrity, as well as my own.

Conversely, you can also sense when a leader is unsound. For example, there was a CFO with whom I worked, who made the board very uneasy. When he presented to the board, he always spoke longer and louder than anyone else. When he answered questions about financial results, he always seemed to be trying to "spin" the numbers as opposed to supporting them with facts. This CFO was intensely focused on the effect that every action and earnings report would have on the price of the company's stock. As a result, he always opposed investments and strategies that might negatively affect the stock price in the short term, even when they might be the right decision for the long term. (The CFO is no longer with the company.)

The CFO in question was not being transparent and his primary focus was not appropriate. A lack of transparency often masks the fact that a leader is not fully competent; an inappropriate focus reflects a dangerous hollowness in his process and attitudes. This is, of course, the exact opposite of the sense of integrity that you would want to convey as a CFO or as any business leader. It also leads us to the third facet of integrity.

Completeness

The third facet of integrity is "the quality or condition of being whole or undivided; completeness." This applies to the catalyst of integrity in two ways:

First, leaders with integrity are themselves whole. They are authentic and genuine as opposed to simply playing a role that does not connect to their true selves. Completeness, like soundness, is a quality that followers can sense in their leaders. As a board member at Wawa Inc., the $3.4 billion chain of company-owned convenience stores centered in the Mid-Atlantic region, I have observed this quality of completeness in Richard D. Wood, Jr., the company's longtime leader who retired in 2004 after 23 years as CEO.

There are no false notes in Dick. When he says customers come first, it is clear that he means it. Whenever a major snowstorm or disaster hits, he is always one of the first people to show up at headquarters or lend a hand at the local stores. It is the same with his emphasis on employee development. Dick does not just say that "seeing people grow, change, and develop" is the most enjoyable part of his job; he makes a point of filling positions by promoting employees whenever possible. Wawa's executive offices are filled with people who started working in the stores. Further, even though over 100 members of Dick's extended family have ownership stakes in the company through trusts, if they want to work there, Dick says, "I just tell them they've got to come to work in the stores and that we post job openings every week. They can apply for jobs based on the openings."

Second, leaders with integrity see and manage their companies in a holistic way, as whole entities. Remember the discussion of systems thinking in Chapter 1? Systems thinking is one manifestation of this hallmark of integrity.

Completeness is also recognizing and considering the effects of your decisions on your company's extended family: its owners, employees (or associates, using Wawa's terminology), customers, suppliers, and the local, national, and global communities in which it operates. To return to Wawa, for a moment, a good example is Dick Wood's response to a salmonella outbreak that occurred in Pennsylvania several years ago. When people began to get sick after eating sandwiches purchased at a competing chain of convenience stores, Dick ordered that all the sandwiches be pulled from the shelves of the Wawa stores in the region until the cause was determined and he was sure that customers could safely consume them. Like Dick, a leader of integrity follows the Golden Rule when it comes to stakeholders by "doing unto others as you would have them do unto you."

THE DEMANDS OF INTEGRITY

The catalytic power of integrity to help you fit in and stand out requires constant development and maintenance. Some of the FISO Factor catalysts are like bank accounts: You can withdraw funds, and later replenish them without doing any serious damage. Integrity is not one of these. You cannot be a leader of some integrity. It is like being pregnant—you either are or you are not.

When I think back on people who worked for me whom I trusted implicitly, they are often people who demonstrated their integrity in small ways. One assistant told me she could not copy a chapter of a library book for me because it violated copyright laws (an issue that had never occurred to me until that time). Another staff member was dismayed to discover that our office's supply of pens and tape disappeared more quickly around the holidays. Because these two employees responded to relatively minor incidents with integrity, I believed that I could trust them to handle more critical tasks in the same way. They fit in and created secure positions for themselves.

Total integrity is especially important when it comes to standing-out. The ultimate act of standing-out when it comes to integrity is publicly exposing corporate wrongdoing. Whistle-blowing is never easy, but it becomes exponentially more difficult if your own integrity can be called into question.

Joseph Bourgart learned this lesson the hard way. In 2002, as CFO of a New Jersey-based medical-equipment maker Vital Signs, Inc., Bourgart believed that the company was overvaluing assets, such as inventory and a Chinese investment, and undervaluing expenses, such as rebates and taxes. He tried to resolve the problems internally, notifying the CEO, the audit committee, and the firm's general counsel approximately thirty times. However, as CFO, he also approved and released the questionable financial results.

In January 2003, Bourgart was forced to resign after the company found that he had "anonymously forwarded confidential corporate information to an investor." At that point he discovered that because he had certified the company's financial results he was not protected under the whistle-blower statutes and, in fact, could be prosecuted under Sarbanes-Oxley for knowingly signing the allegedly erroneous reports. In compromising his own integrity, Bourgart found himself tarred with the same brush.

Eventually, Deloitte and Touche investigated Vital Signs accounting practices. In December 2003, Touche announced it had found no evidence of illegal practices, but the company did take a charge of 40 cents per share to "correct concerns." Bourgart eventually sued the company under New Jersey law; the suit was settled out of court in July 2004.

ST. IGNATIUS'S TEST

There are many simple ways to test the integrity of your decisions. There is the "New York Times" test: How would you feel if your decision were reported on the front page of the *Times*? Another test that I like is the "Grandmother" test, which asks what your grandmother would say about your decisions. And, over 400 years ago, in 1535, St. Ignatius of Loyola, the founder of the Jesuit Order, created a measure of integrity that has stood the test of time. He formulated a series of rules to follow when "making elections" that include:

• Is your decision in accordance with your religious beliefs?
• Are you willing to live up to the dictates of your decision; if you are making a decision that includes others, would you be willing to do what you are asking of them?

- If you were on the point of death, would you make the same decision?
- If it were Judgment Day, would you be comfortable defending your decision?

St. Ignatius's rules reflect his own priorities and concerns. They offer an example of how you can use factors beyond the law as a basis for judgment, as well as to test whether you have been "impaired" by your employment context and whether you are acting consistently with your values.

In addition to constant vigilance over their integrity, aspiring leaders must also realize that the bar of integrity fluctuates. Ethics are often determined by society at large. But society changes over time and thus, so do ethics. What may have been acceptable behavior in one period may well be scoffed at and perhaps, even illegal in another. Further, the bar of integrity rises in times like these, when wrongdoing appears to be more prevalent than usual. Dean of the Yale School of Management Jeffrey Sonnenfeld notes that it is not only those business leaders who were guilty of fraud and other crimes who have suffered recently. In December 2003, he pointed out a "new pattern of CEO exits that include the recent departures of Boeing's Phil Condit, Delta's Leo Mullin, NYSE's Richard Grasso, AMR Corp.'s Don Carty, and Sprint's Bill Esrey." These were respected, high-performing leaders who did nothing illegal. What did they do? They were all indirectly linked to scandals, or as in the case of Grasso, were judged to have violated today's ethical standards at some earlier date. As a result, says Sonnefeld: "Each of these leaders sadly lost the legitimacy to lead because they lost their moral authority."

The bar of integrity also rises according to your position and the position of your company. This is a lesson that some companies learn the hard way. Microsoft's aggressive style of business was much applauded when the company was younger and smaller. But, as the world's leading software company, with 2004 sales of $36.8 billion, aggressive business practices appear less protective and more monopolistic. After years of legal wrangling, the company's leaders have begun to take this lesson to heart.

So too has Wal-Mart Stores, Inc. Wal-Mart, the world's largest retailer, reported revenues of $256 billion in 2004, but it is coming under increasing fire for its treatment of employees and its negative impact on communities. This is a situation that has not gone unnoticed by its leaders. In the 2004 annual report, CEO Lee Scott writes:

> As the largest, and possibly most visible, company in the world, we are being held to an increasingly higher standard of behavior. Our financial performance is an important measure by which we are judged, but it is no longer the only measure. Our Customers, our Associates, the Communities in which we do business and the general public expect more of us. In the past, we were judged mainly by our accomplishments. Today, Wal-Mart is increasingly defined by our actions as an employer, corporate citizen and business partner. We must always do the right things in the right way.

ORGANIZATIONAL INTEGRITY

People judge the integrity of leaders by the actions of their companies as well as by their personal actions. Further, senior leaders may face personal legal liability for the actions of their companies. Therefore, organizational integrity is as important as personal integrity to aspiring leaders.

A breach in organizational integrity can jeopardize the careers and lives of all employees. Take, for example, the collapse of Arthur

Andersen & Company, an event that stunned many people including me. My first job after finishing my MBA was with Andersen, and the financial discipline and professional integrity I learned there has always served me well. This was a company of sterling reputation, which devoted 10 percent of its gross revenue to training. Yet, when just a single Andersen partner was indicted in the Enron scandal, the company ceased to exist.

Creating an intense organizational focus on integrity can help to avoid the draconian consequences that Andersen experienced. FISO Factor leaders work hard to implant a sense of responsibility and accountability in all employees. Responsibility means that you have a developed sense of right and wrong, one that will guide you to "do the right thing" and "do things right." Accountability means that you own the decision and recognize that you must pay the costs if it fails. These costs can include financial remuneration, devoting time and effort to rebuild a reputation, and even in some situations, a public apology. Certainly, companies that have survived incidents of wrongdoing have learned that lesson. At MCI (formerly Worldcom), recently appointed chief ethics officer Nancy Higgins hired the University of Virginia and New York University to provide ethics training education to 55,000 employees to "help them understand the line between aggressive business practice and improper activity." Abbott Laboratories, which paid a $600 million fine in 2003 after employees were caught coaching customers how to overbill Medicaid and Medicare in an FBI sting operation, now uses a touch screen video game to teach employees ethical and legal business practices.

FOUR INTEGRITY MYTHS

In his study of reputational capital, Fordham University professor Kevin Jackson found that reputation is driven by other people's perceptions of your character, and that character itself is formed by integrity and fair play. He also dispels four common myths about integrity and fair play:

Myth 1: Our morals and ethics are formed at an early age and cannot be changed.

Reality: Studies show that moral education programs are more likely to change adults than children and that moral development continues with age.

Myth 2: Integrity is an individual choice and is unaffected by organizations.

Reality: Research proves that individual behavior is strongly influenced by authority figures and organizational context.

Myth 3: People are basically ethical, so they do not require moral education.

Reality: Studies suggest that people have radically different ideas of what is right and wrong.

Myth 4: Ethics are not relevant to business and, further, are an anchor on organizational performance.

Reality: Studies show that customers and employees prefer to deal with companies that are honest and trustworthy and that respect them.

Employee education is not the only support for organizational integrity; the corporate culture must be willing to hear unwelcome news. Leaders must maintain open avenues for dissent and for whistle-blowing. As one of Wawa's store managers says, "If you listen to the whispers, you won't ever have to listen to the screams." Sarbanes-Oxley has provisions aimed at breaking what ex-Senator Tom Daschle called "the corporate code of silence," but if the corporate culture encourages honest communication, does not punish naysayers, and addresses problems at early stages, it may well be that ethical lapses will be few and far between.

Silence is the enemy of integrity. Harvard Business School professor Leslie Perlow finds a "vicious spiral of silence" in many of the companies she studies. "People silence themselves because they want to be seen as accommodating and hardworking. They think that by staying silent they can speed things up or preserve relationships," she says. Instead, their "unwillingness to speak up [has] trapped them all in dysfunctional behavior." This is why FISO Factor leaders encourage factual, open, and honest communication. They tell the truth with appropriate directness, do not shirk difficult issues, and deliver bad news when they must. In doing so they provide a model for others and support organizational honesty and integrity.

INTEGRITY YIELDS TRUST

Aspiring business leaders do not win their positions in democratic elections nor are they raised by general acclaim. They are appointed. Nevertheless, until they demonstrate the integrity necessary to earn and maintain the trust of their followers, they cannot truly claim their appointed places.

Without integrity and trust, aspiring leaders cannot fit in. Further, leaders cannot generate the support required to pursue new initiatives and transform their companies unless they are trusted by their followers. Thus, integrity also creates the trust that leaders rely on to stand out. The spectrum below illustrates how the catalyst of integrity relates to the FISO Factor.

John Carl, who served as CFO at Amoco Corporation and The Allstate Corporation before his retirement in 2002, is a fine illustration of how trust supports a leader's FISO Factor. Early in John's career, he was working as a plant accountant when his boss's boss visited the location. Alone with John, this intimidating executive began to ask his opinion of various people on the staff and for whom he worked. John was polite and

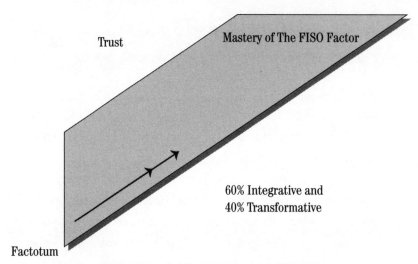

Figure 5-1   The Catalytic Spectrum for Integrity

spoke of each person in positive and supportive terms. The executive became visibly impatient, and finally said, "I don't want to hear what you think I want to hear. I want to hear your honest assessment of these people." John proceeded to respond fully and honestly. Impressed by John's perceptions, the executive became a mentor to him and helped promote him through the organization. John told me this story as an example of how the executive's trust in John's integrity had helped him fit in.

I worked with John later in his career when he was controller at Kraft Foods, Inc. When Philip Morris Companies, Inc., acquired Kraft, John was ordered to undertake a massive reduction in the finance and accounting staff in order to meet the targeted cost savings. After surveying the required cuts, John said that he could not cut the staff as deep as the mandate and still complete the work required of his department in the consolidation. He offered to resign if there was no other option. CEO Michael Miles supported John's assessment, saying, "If John says he can't cut this deeply, I believe him and know to trust him." John's integrity also created the trust that enabled him to stand up and stand out.

THE ABCS OF INTEGRITY

Here are some thought-starter questions for integrity.

Fitting In with Integrity

Attitude: Believe integrity is a business imperative. What role does integrity play in your mental image of your company and career? How does integrity support your personal reputation? your organization's reputation?

Behavior: Act in accordance with ethical standards. What are the standards for integrity in your company? in your industry? in your profession? How can you alter your management style to better reflect those standards?

Characteristic: Encourage honest and open communication. How can you encourage subordinates to speak out about ethical concerns? What new avenues of communication can you open in your sphere of responsibility?

Standing Out with Integrity

Attitude: Bring your whole self to work. What parts of your personality do you hide at work? How can you release them to become a more authentic leader?

Behavior: Be ready to say "no" if necessary. How can you ensure that ethical considerations are fully explored without alienating others? What are the ethical boundaries that you would sacrifice your career to maintain?

Characteristic: Seek out the extended ethical implications. How will your decisions be judged by stakeholders with differing ethical standards? How can you apply those standards to reach better decisions and build your reputational capital?

CHAPTER

$$\boxed{6}$$

LINKAGES: THE LEVER OF ALLIANCE

No one knows who discovered the lever; its use dates to man's pre-history. Archimedes of Syracuse is credited with the first mathematical articulation of the law of the lever over 2,200 years ago. While most of us probably cannot recite Archimedes' formula, we do remember the colorful challenge he issued to communicate its power: "Give me where to stand, and I will move the earth."

Leaders, too, can use a lever to move their worlds. It is the lever of alliance. In this case, alliance means more than a formal partnership between companies. When we talk about the lever of alliance, we are talking about the entire network of relationships that surround leaders and their companies. These linkages include all of the bonds, ties, and associations, both formal and informal, which connect us to one another.

Linkages, the connections that make up networks, are the third catalytic agent of the FISO Factor. The power potential of linkages lies in their depth and reach, and most importantly, in the two-way flow of information, services, and resources which streams through them. This power represents a critical factor in the pursuit of both organizational and career success.

The connections between people have been a topic of interest to sociologists, but in the past decade, driven by the quest to understand the mechanics behind the phenomenal growth rate of the Internet, this interest has spread into many other fields, including business. The previously intangible advantage of linkages is now being quantified as *social capital*, a term that University of Michigan School of Business professor Wayne Baker simply defines as "the resources available in and through personal and business networks."

Baker ascribes significant advantages to people who enjoy high levels of social capital: better jobs, better pay and promotions, greater influence and effectiveness, and even happiness, health, and a longer life. Companies with high levels of social capital, he says, are offered more venture capital and financing, learn and execute better, attract more customers with less marketing, find better strategic partners, and are less susceptible to hostile takeover attempts. This may sound like snake oil, but, as we'll see throughout this chapter, the power of linkages is well supported by quantitative and qualitative evidence.

Linkages play a critical role in the work of fitting-in and standing-out. In fact, the catalytic agent of linkages is the only one that applies equally to both tasks. Each of the FISO Factor agents has important applications to both tasks, but usually in unequal measure. Unlike the other agents, the agent of linkages is applied to the work of standing-out as often as it is applied to the work of fitting-in. See Figure 6-1.

For instance, linkages provide an essential catalyst in the ability to fit in at a new job. I was well traveled by the time I accepted the CFO position at BIC, but in addition to being the fulfillment of dream, a C-level position in BIC's Paris headquarters also presented a daunting cultural challenge. Thierry Benoit and his family helped me meet that

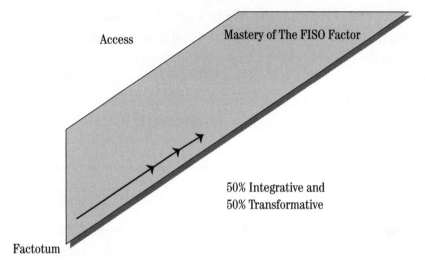

Figure 6-1   The Catalytic Spectrum for Linkages

challenge. Thierry is a partner at accounting firm Deloitte Touche Tohmatsu, and he was the leader of Deloitte's team at BIC. As part of his job, he gave me a thorough education in France's accounting and regulatory requirements. He helped me to fit in professionally.

My professional link with Thierry evolved into a personal one. We became friends and Thierry invited me to spend time with members of his family. They guided me through the nuances of French culture and etiquette. With their help, I was able to fit in socially. This is no small matter. "Indeed," explains Suzanne Fairlie, president of executive retained search firm ProSearch, Inc., "the number one reason most people leave jobs in their first year of employment is related to culture: the person has the right skills, the right experience, but not the right cultural fit, so s/he doesn't fit in, is not happy, and thus not productive."

Linkages just as quickly proved to be an essential element for successfully standing-out at BIC. Thierry and his team played an important role in resolving the problem of the balance sheet that did not balance at BIC (see the discussion in Chapter 5). They endorsed my decision to delay earnings, an important factor when it came time for me to notify the chairman of the company. As a new CFO, literally an alien, who was forced to stand out just a few short weeks after her arrival, I had not yet had the time to establish my own credibility within the company. But, the linkages with Deloitte's team lent critical support to my recommendation. It was not just a new hire from America who advocated delay, but also Deloitte's respected professionals.

THE COMPETITIVE ADVANTAGE OF LINKAGES

One reason that Lewis Carroll's *Alice's Adventures in Wonderland* provides an intriguing allegory for businesspeople is that it suggests how difficult a career without linkages can be. Alice has no relationships in Wonderland; she is on her own. Without trusted guides, she must rely on experiential learning to understand this new world and she must endure all of the painful mistakes that learning-by-doing can entail. Aspiring leaders who do not develop linkages are in much the same position: They must work harder and they are more vulnerable to error.

Conversely, there are leaders who seem to enjoy great luck. They always seem to be in the right place at the right time with the right skills to capitalize on this serendipity. Often, however, what appears to be serendipity is actually the competitive advantage of a robust network of linkages. Linkages produce opportunity, creativity, and productivity.

Opportunity

Linkages open the door to opportunity. Whether it is a new job with greater responsibility and reward potential, a high profile assignment within your company, or a lucrative business contract, who you know is as instrumental as *what* you know in producing opportunities. When opportunities seem to seek us out, instead of vice versa, there is a good chance linkages are at work.

This has certainly been proved repeatedly throughout my career. In one instance, linkages provided me access to a job that had been previously denied me. In August 1990, I was happily employed at Kraft when a recruiter called about a position with Sara Lee. After speaking to my immediate boss about his view of my future, a view that was disappointingly nebulous, I decided to pursue this new opportunity. (There is another lesson here: Never decide to leave a job without first exploring your current employer's plans for your future. Sometimes the greener side of the fence is the side you are on.)

I passed all the preliminaries and had a positive interview with Sara Lee's president. Subsequently, a full day of interviews was scheduled, including a meeting with Sara Lee's chairman, John Bryan. Then came an unexpected call; the interviews were canceled and five months into the process, I was told there would be no job offer. It turned out that Sara Lee had recently hired several Kraft executives and Kraft had fired a retaliatory legal volley to stop the poaching.

A month after this disappointment in January 1991, I attended a member's meeting at the Chicago Council on Foreign Relations, where John Bryan introduced the speaker. After the lunch and the speech, I introduced myself to John. It took him a moment to recognize my name and our connection, but we had an interesting talk about global issues in the food business, the speaker's topic. The next day, I received a call from the recruiter; Sara Lee's interest had been revived. Shortly afterwards, I was hired as executive director, business planning. The external linkage of membership in the Foreign Relations council had opened a door that once had been sealed tight.

Creativity

Creativity is often seen as a mysterious process driven by serendipity and lightning bolts of inspiration. People often say they are not creative, attributing such a talent to an eccentric or lucky person who happens to be at the right place at the right time. For instance, Archimedes realized that water displacement could be used to measure volume while taking a bath. In the excitement of his discovery, he reportedly jumped up and ran naked through the streets of Syracuse, yelling, "Eureka!" It is easy to see from Archimedes's behavior how creativity could be mistaken for a lightning bolt, but in fact, he had made a mental connection between a job he had been assigned (to ensure the King's new crown was made of solid gold) and the change in water level as he entered the bath. It is connections like these that often generate creativity and innovation. Plus, if you reflect upon the problem needed to be solved, think about it in various situations, and keep an open playful mind, remarkable possibilities start to come to mind.

Linkages are an important source of creative connections. "The usual image of creativity is that it's some sort of a genetic gift, some heroic act," says Ronald Burt. "But creativity is an import-export game. It's not a creation game." In 2001, Burt studied a group of 673 supply chain managers at aerospace and defense contractor Raytheon Company. He asked the managers to offer one idea for improving the supply chain and also to describe with whom they had discussed the idea. He received 455 ideas and asked two senior executives to evaluate them. When Burt correlated the results, he found that managers with networks that extended beyond their functional units (beyond what he calls "structural holes") were more likely to express and discuss an idea, offer an idea that gained the attention of senior management, and produce a valuable idea. Burt writes:

> People with connections across structural holes have early access to diverse, often contradictory, information and interpretations which gives them a competitive advantage in seeing and developing good ideas. People connected to groups beyond their own can expect to find themselves delivering valuable ideas, seeming to be gifted with creativity.

Thus, the breadth of an aspiring leader's linkages is directly related to his ability to create and innovate. These linkages, particularly when they connect us to new groups, are the pathways on which ideas travel. When a leader opens new paths, she gains access to new ideas and increases the chances of creating "Eureka" moments of her own.

Productivity

The catalytic agent of linkages also has a strong positive effect on personal and organizational productivity. Think about how ideas are approved, projects are assigned, and work is accomplished within your company. If it is anything like the companies I have worked in, there are fixed procedures and functional experts through which these activities flow. Frequently the process can appear to be bureaucratic and not efficient. Linkages can help speed movement within the company and ultimately, to the customer. Sometimes, linkages can even enable you to bypass prescribed but non-value-added procedures altogether by providing direct access to the resources needed to accomplish your goals.

Often, the linkages that can best bolster your productivity are internal linkages to what Art Kleiner, the director of research at strategic change consulting firm Dialogos LLC, calls "core groups." Every company has a core group, says Kleiner, that is, the group of people "who really matter" and serve as the source of the company's energy, drive, and direction. Further, a leader's success and failure is intimately connected to the company's core group, so the quality of the linkages you create with them is critical.

The recognition of the importance of internal linkages is one of the driving factors in the growth of "onboarding" coaches, defined as career consultants who help new executives fit into their companies. Judi Glova hired such a coach to advise her when she started her new job as director of public affairs at Roche Pharmaceuticals. Glova, according to *The Wall Street Journal*, "learned to identify players with the power to block her ideas, for example. She spent extra time getting acquainted with them before their meetings and deliberately sat beside them during lunch. Today, those colleagues help with her requests."

Sometimes external linkages will be the key to increased productivity. When the Hannaford Bros. Co. supermarket chain was put up for sale, it was my responsibility, as CFO, to ensure that the sale and acquisition process was properly conducted. I had been involved in acquisitions before, but not at this level. So, the first call I made was to John Carl, my former colleague at Kraft Foods, who was now my friend of over 15 years. John had been CFO at Amoco throughout its merger with British Petroleum. He rounded out my knowledge, kindly explaining the fine points of the process and alerting me to potential sticking points, such as the sensitivities involved in sharing financial information with suitors who were also competitors. The linkage with John gave me the competence and courage to successfully manage the acquisition process.

CREATING AND MAINTAINING LINKAGES

Breadth and depth are *not* mutually exclusive when it comes to the catalytic agent of linkages. I am amused by the competitions that sometimes ensue when people whip out their PDAs. It quickly becomes a matter of pride as to who has the most "people" stuffed into them. I know one person who has over 3,000 contacts in his PDA; I read about another with 6,000 contacts in her network. Unfortunately for "people" counters, the value of an aspiring leader's network is a function of not only the breadth but the *depth* of the linkages. The depth—that is, the meaningfulness and frequency—of your linkages is as crucial as the breadth—the quantity and reach—of your linkages.

To be sure breadth is important. As Ronald Burt's work discussed earlier has proved, the greater reach of your linkages, the greater the chance that they will provide an information advantage. The quantity aspect of your network is evident by the number of people who are aware of and use your network. Robert Metcalfe, cofounder of 3Com Corporation and a pioneer in computer networking, postulates that usefulness of a network equals the square of its number of users. Metcalfe's law, which has been applied to fax machines and computers, also applies to personal and organizational networks. The more linkages in your network, the greater its potential utility becomes.

Depth plays just as important a role as breadth in the development of linkages. Networkers often fail because they miss this lesson. They are so busy distributing their business cards and counting contacts that they tend to forget that meaningful relationships require more than a perfunctory handshake and a periodic hello. For a linkage to have depth, it must be a connection that offers value to both parties. It must also offer some degree of intimacy; linkages are made between people, not business cards.

So how do you create and maintain a robust network of linkages that feature both breadth and depth? Here are three guidelines to keep in mind:

- Create a robust network of linkages.
- Focus on giving instead of getting.
- Practice the "touch-tone approach" to linkages.

Create a Robust Network of Linkages

We tend not to recognize the breadth and depth of our potential linkages. Most of us are members of multiple social clusters, each of which contains multiple linkage points.

Start by thinking about the many potential linkages within your own company. The relationships that you create at work are among the most important when it comes to leadership effectiveness. As Bill

George, the former CEO of Medtronic, Inc., says, "The capacity to develop close and enduring relationships is one mark of a leader."

Keep in mind that your linkages at work need not be direct connections based on your job and counted as how many people report to you or how many people you must serve. In fact, it is often better if they are not direct subordinates or bosses. I stumbled upon a valuable set of informal linkages when I joined an aerobics class at Hannaford Bros. Co. Eight of us attended the class on Monday, Wednesday, and Friday at 6:30 a.m. Because I was not wearing my CFO hat, it was where I got the "straight skinny" about events at all different levels within the company. I was just another class member and we sweated and talked together as equals.

Think about linkages at previous employers. It is always surprising how many people leave their relationships behind when they leave jobs. As you have already seen through the earlier example of my relationship with John Carl, those linkages have been extremely important in my career. I have also discovered that after leaving a job, relationships with former colleagues often become deeper and more intimate. We are no longer constrained by the corporate hierarchy and the power dynamic that exists in all companies.

At my sadly defunct former employer Arthur Andersen, former employees were never shunned. They became honored alumni, and the firm held annual meetings to bring them together with the current employees. The company, like other consulting firms, such as McKinsey, understood that their alumni network was a valuable source of information and future business.

Speaking of alumni, your academic affiliations are the next valuable source of linkages. In my case, the relationships with students, alumni, professors, and administrators at Northwestern University and the Kellogg School of Management are among the most meaningful relationships in my life. (I met my husband at Northwestern.) For 25 years, I served as the representative from my class at Kellogg, and in various capacities on the boards and alumni associations of both schools. After all this time, the opportunities that grew from these roots are impossible to count.

Professional affiliations can be as important as academic ones, so become a joiner. There are professional groups of virtually every ilk. Join at least two: the most active group in your industry and the most active in your chosen profession. If at all feasible, volunteer to serve on their boards or operating committees. The people you meet and the skills and knowledge you gain will repay your efforts many times over.

Create links in your community. Explore the opportunities to serve in governmental and philanthropic organizations. Meg Weston, the former CEO of Konica North America, described the benefits of participation best when she said, "Through those avenues I have found innumerable resources—CEOs facing similar business problems of employee recruitment, financing, downsizing, or whatever . . . people who can provide or direct me to people with specific expertise that I need at some time."

DON'T UNDERESTIMATE THE STRENGTH OF WEAK TIES

In 1973, the *American Journal of Sociology* published an article by a young assistant professor named Mark Granovetter that would become one of the most influential in its field. Titled "The Strength of Weak Ties," it made the counterintuitive argument that weak ties—those linkages with people who are outside our immediate circles—were often more valuable sources than strong ties—linkages with direct associates at work, close friends, and family.

"I saw an important undeveloped theme," says Granovetter, who is now chairman of Stanford University's

Sociology Department, "that weak ties were crucial for individuals' instrumental needs and for overall social cohesiveness. This idea was reinforced by my knowledge of analogous physical phenomena: weak hydrogen bonds that hold together large molecules, and weak forces in particle physics."

Granovetter tested his thinking by studying how people find jobs. What he found supported his theory: People did not tend to find jobs through strong ties, because people linked by strong ties usually share the same sources and knowledge. Instead, jobs often come to us through our weak ties with those acquaintances who travel in circles other than our own.

The lesson: Do not neglect the development of linkages with people outside your "social clusters." They can extend your reach to resources far beyond your immediate ken.

Focus on Giving Instead of Getting

My favorite French verb is *partager*. It means "to share" and it takes us to the heart of linkages. Relationships are built on sharing, the two-way flow of conversation, and caring. People who approach linkages solely, or even primarily, focused on "what's in it for me" quickly find out that the answer is "very little."

The best linkages are built on mutual benefit, but the best way to *start* a relationship is to be the first to provide a benefit. Consider it an investment in the future. Sometimes, like any risk, the investment may not grow as you had hoped, but the ones that do grow will more than cover your losses.

If you are reluctant to give before you get, consider the experience of Anna Belyaev, CEO and cofounder of e-learning company Type A Multimedia and a Russian immigrant. Instead of asking for favors from others when she started her company, Belyaev decided to do favors for others, at least five per week. As a result, she says, "I've got leads coming out of my ears. It's part of my prospecting plan that I introduce other people and provide them with leads. Then you feel you can count on them to do the same. It's a kind of barter-exchange."

The time and effort that you invest in helping others and developing your linkages is also an effective hedge against future emergencies. Today, business moves very quickly and when you need help, there is often not enough time to create a new linkage. Existing linkages and past favors go a long way toward remedying such situations.

NETWORKING TACTICS

The Pepsi Bottling Group clearly recognizes the role that linkages play in leadership effectiveness. In July 2004, the company brought its 100 top diverse leaders from the United States and Canada to Greenwich, CT, for a conference focused on building their personal networks. Here are some of the tips they learned:

- Use your strong ties to help you break into new circles.
- Set aside time for activities that broaden your network.
- All encounters are opportunities for expanding and diversifying your network.
- Build ties before you need them.
- Understand your contacts' interests and concerns, know what they value.
- Have something to trade, give back to the network.

Practice the "Touch-Tone Approach" to Linkages

It always pays to be sensitive when you utilize your linkages. There are two qualities that characterize these contacts: touch—the medium that is best for the contact; and tone—how you express yourself. First, think about the touch. Are you going to send letters and emails (low touch) or do you find phone calls or an invitation to lunch (high touch) more effective? Then, consider how you plan to interact with another person, using a particular tone. Will you take a more traditional route and wait until an individual needs something and asks you? Or will you use an innovative approach and ask someone to become involved in a committee or special group? Perhaps, you want a heavy tone and will ask directly for an introduction or assistance.

Even though we always like to think a light touch and light tone will be enough for the receiver to know what we have to offer, there are times when that will not break through and reach the decision maker, for example in a consulting proposal. Given the urgency of your needs and the situation of the person with whom you have a linkage, the heavier touch and tone may be more appropriate.

Someone who is a master of using the right touch and tone at the appropriate time is Dick Lochridge. Dick, who is the founder of Lochridge & Company, strategic change advisers, was a director at Hannaford Bros. Co. when we first met. After I moved to BIC, I got a friendly note from Dick. He was planning to visit Paris and wondered if we might get together (light touch/light tone). In the letter, almost as an aside, he mentioned that he would also like to meet Bruno Bich, if it was convenient. We discussed dates and Dick came to Paris. We had a wonderful visit and by chance, Bruno was available, so I introduced Dick to my boss (heavy touch/light tone). Several months later, BIC was considering an acquisition. We decided we needed some expert help with modeling and integration strategy. We decided to engage Lochridge & Co. because of Dick's earlier, albeit brief, introduction. Clearly during the engagement, we had ample time to work on tough issues together (heavy touch/heavy tone). From the initial light touch and tone, we created a profitable linkage.

Dick's contact stands in stark contrast to an email I recently received from another longtime acquaintance, also a consultant. I had not heard from him in a couple of years and his purpose in writing was clearly career-oriented. He was finishing an engagement, he wrote, and was looking for another. As an aside in this email he asked about me and my current situation: "How were things going?" he asked before signing off. I took no pleasure in replying.

There are times when a heavy tone or touch is warranted. If you are facing a crisis and need to act quickly, you should say so and explain why. But you should only have to use a heavy touch and tone occasionally. The rest of the time it pays to put yourself in your contact's shoes and edit your touch and tone accordingly.

THE LINKED ORGANIZATION

Unsurprisingly, the catalytic agent of linkages has organizational as well as individual application. In the past, companies could get away with being insular. In the post-WWII economic boom when consumer demand soared, for instance, close connections to markets and customers did not seem all that important, innovation could be postponed, and the competition was not quite so fierce. Companies could close their doors and concentrate on doing the same things that had worked in the past. Today, however, any company that cuts itself off from the rest of world is following a prescription for disaster.

Companies that act as if they are closed networks face distinct dangers. They are vulnerable to groupthink and other barriers to rational decision making. They have little idea of what is happening beyond their borders, of how their markets, competitors, and regulatory environments are evolving. They cannot tap into the resources and creativity of their suppliers and other strategic partners. They cannot connect to their customers. They stagnate. When Ronald Burt studied closed networks, he concluded "that network closure does not facilitate trust so much as it amplifies predispositions, creating a structural arthritis in which people cannot learn what they do not already know."

The application of social networking to business organizations is a new, but rapidly emerging, field. At this point some theories on the importance of social networking have been confirmed through a few early "wins," but this field is sure to be a topic of great interest to leaders in the near future, particularly those who want to avoid fates such as "structural arthritis." See the sidebar on "viral marketing," in the case of 3M and the book *In Search of Excellence*.

THE SECRET BEHIND VIRAL MARKETING

Linkages are the secret behind the new strategy of viral marketing. Viral marketing is a guerilla marketing technique that depends on influential trendsetters and early adopters to spread the word about products and services. It works because when its messages catch on, they career and echo through ever greater numbers of linkages and ever more distant networks, spreading the word to potential customers around the globe.

Although viral marketing is a new strategy, it has been used in the past. In 1980, 3M used it to launch the ubiquitous Post-it note. The company's marketers astutely enlisted the help of the secretary of the chairman, who tapped her professional linkages and sent free samples to C-level secretaries throughout the Fortune 500. Post-its quickly became one of the top five office supply products in the country.

In 1982, Tom Peters and Bob Waterman again demonstrated the viral marketing power of linkages when they launched their book, *In Search of Excellence*. The two men used McKinsey & Company's linkages to distribute over 15,000 copies of the draft manuscript throughout Corporate America. The book's publishers were reportedly stunned; Peters and Waterman had given away more copies than they had anticipated selling. The tactic, however, created unprecedented demand and by 1999, *In Search of Excellence* had sold over 4.5 million copies in the United States alone.

One of the major issues that has emerged is the widespread ignorance regarding the many internal linkages that already exist within companies. These too often go unrecognized and untapped. University of Michigan professor Wayne Baker and Humax Corporation created one solution to this problem: a training exercise that they call the "reciprocity ring." In the exercise, each participant makes a specific request for help from the entire the group, which then attempts to fulfill the request through their linkages. How well does it work? When Baker facilitated a reciprocity ring with 30 managers in a global engineering firm, he reported, "the reciprocity experience generated more than 200 individual acts of contribution worth (according to the engineers who participated) $261,400 and a savings of 1,244 hours."

In another example of how existing linkages can be tapped, 3i Group, a venture capital firm, installed a social networking software package that connected its 800 employees in 16 countries. This software application enabled a company team in Spain that was on the trail of a leveraged buyout opportunity to locate fellow employees in Germany who had connections with the target company's parent, also a German company. The resulting deal earned the 3i Group $100 million.

A second issue to keep in mind is relationship valuation. Valuing linkages is a difficult task. Like knowledge, they are intangible assets.

Nevertheless, they are differentiable by their quality and by what they enable an organization to accomplish. Further, as we saw in Chapter 4, whenever a company plans to invest capital, it must be able to quantify the return on that investment.

The problem is that the experiences of Wayne Baker and the 3i Group are more the exception than the rule. In 2001, I researched this topic with Danny Ertel and Jeff Weiss of Vantage Partners, a consulting firm with expertise in building corporate relationship management capabilities. We found that few companies had institutionalized relationship management capabilities. Thus, most cannot properly value their ROR—return on relationships.

ROR compares the benefits of accomplishments produced by what the relationship enables companies to do that would have been less, poorer quality, or slower had there been no relationship. Further, ROR enables companies to focus on resolving relationship issues in a coherent and rigorous way.

Business problems require business solutions and relationship problems require relationship solutions. A problem with trust, for example, cannot be remedied by a reduction in fees. By measuring ROR, companies can avoid leaving relationship management to chance. After all, one of the truisms of business is "what gets measured, gets done." So, instead of hoping that skilled employees can create a relationship that is profitable, companies can ensure that all the ingredients for successful linkage are present.

The final issue to consider is the so-called keystone advantage, a topic discussed in the 2004 book *The Keystone Advantage* by Harvard Business School professor Marco Iansiti and consultant Roy Levien. They write that today's business world is increasingly characterized by networks composed of multiple companies. Accordingly, the ultimate competitive advantage is becoming a keystone in these networks—that is, a company that serves as a central connector (a hub) in a network.

Iansiti and Levien point to companies such as IBM, Wal-Mart, and Microsoft to make their case. Hundreds and thousands of companies are part of the networks of these corporate keystones. Thus, to a large extent, the success of keystone companies, like Microsoft, is dependent not only on the management of their internal elements but also on the management of the external linkages in their networks. "Strategy," say the authors, "is becoming, to an increasing extent, the art of managing assets one does not own."

This is the catalytic agent of linkages interpreted in macro terms. If your company's success is predicated on the performance of its network, then the health and effectiveness of all of the companies with which it is linked become a legitimate concern. Thus, you can be sure that leadership success in the future will be dependent on how well you can manage the organizational linkages on which these networks are built.

LINKAGES YIELD ACCESS

The catalyst of linkages opens the doors to infinite possibilities for your career and company. Its yield is *access*. Your linkages smooth the way for you to fit in at your company; they create the access you need to make a secure place for yourself. Your linkages also create the access to the opportunities, ideas, and ever-greater levels of productivity that you need to stand out.

Linkages provide one more thing: the pathways through which learning flows into and throughout organizations. Learning is a FISO Factor catalyst in and of itself. Now that we have explored the channels through which connections travel and bonds are made, we can turn to how it supports successful careers and companies.

THE ABCS OF LINKAGES

Here are some thought-starter questions for linkages.

Fitting In with Linkages

Attitude: Embrace the human connection. Are you approaching relationships at work with the same zest as your social relationships? Are you focusing on common ground instead of conflict in your business relationships?

Behavior: Seek out and cultivate linkages with "blockers." In your current position, which people tend to react negatively to you and your ideas? How can you cultivate and transform those relationships?

Characteristic: Think in linkage terms. Do you consider the use of linkages as you plan your work? Who do you know who can offer unique insight into your next major decision or task?

Standing Out with Linkages

Attitude: Create tomorrow's linkages today. What skills and resources will you need to be effective after your next promotion or job change? How can you begin to create the linkages that will provide those resources?

Behavior: Constantly extend your network. What groups can you join that span the functional boundaries within your company? What professional organizations offer access to peers working in other industries?

Characteristic: Be honestly interested in helping your peers. What are the needs of your peers at work? How can you use your linkages to help them obtain the resources they need?

7

LEARNING: THE WELLSPRING OF RENEWAL

In 1513, Juan Ponce, better remembered as Ponce de Leon, decided to search for the Fountain of Youth. In his fifties, the Spanish conquistador was already rich from earlier conquests and a stint as royal governor of Puerto Rico, but he was not content to retire quietly. Instead, he set out in March to conquer new lands and find the fabled wellspring that could restore health and revitalize the aged. Ponce sailed from Puerto Rico with three ships fitted out at his own expense. A month later, he "discovered" and claimed for Spain a new land that he named *La Florida*. He searched Florida and the Bahamas for the Fountain of Youth, but of course, he never found the legendary waters.

Everyone ages, but we all know people who never seem to get old. Sure, they have wrinkles and gray hair, but because they also have a sparkle in their eyes and active, open minds, we tend not to perceive them as "old." How do these people retain their youthful countenance?

Often, it is their interest in the world, their curiosity. They have discovered a wellspring of renewal that drives passion, alertness, and spirit. It is a love of learning.

Peter Drucker, who turned 95 in 2004, is a notable example of a lifelong learner. He pursues knowledge with a vigor that puts people a quarter of his age to shame. In 1929, after the Great Crash, Drucker lost his job in a Frankfurt brokerage firm and, at age 20, found another position as a financial and foreign affairs reporter at the city's largest newspaper. As a journalist, Drucker realized that he needed a broad base of knowledge. He explains:

> So I began to force myself to study afternoons and evenings: international relations and international law; the history of social and legal institutions; finance; and so on. Gradually, I developed a system. I still adhere to it. Every three or four years I pick a new subject. It may be Japanese art; it may be economic. Three years of study are by no means enough to master a subject, but they are enough to understand it. So for more than 60 years I have kept on studying one subject at a time. That not only has given me a substantial fund of knowledge. It has also forced me to be open to new disciplines and new approaches and new methods—for every one of the subjects I have studied makes different assumptions and employs a different methodology.

This is a portrait of a self-directed learner. When I had the opportunity to hear Drucker speak and meet him, he was 91 years old. At that point, he had been pursuing dedicated topics for approximately seven decades. He had mastered more than 20 subjects, the equivalent of over 20 college degrees! That huge knowledge base is evident in everything Drucker does. He makes connections that others miss; he has a sense of perspective that allows him to properly weigh raw data; and, in his nineties and often in poor health, he has mental energy and purpose. He is a man who is still growing, who embraces the idea that there is still much to learn.

Leadership, like all of life's endeavors, is a process of continuous learning. Aspiring leaders fit in using a process of intraorganizational learning through which they discover how their companies work and what drives them. Learning's greatest application, however, is its ability to drive the process by which aspiring leaders stand out as individuals, and transform their companies. See Figure 7-1.

Learning, which enables you to release the leader within, is the fourth catalytic agent of the FISO Factor. Learning is a wellspring of renewal for business leaders and their organizations. It is the mechanism that enables personal and corporate growth and change, without which our careers and companies would stagnate and eventually die. A popular motivational poster shows a line of horses following behind another horse with the phrase "If you are not leading, the view never changes." That view reminds me of why releasing the leader within is so important. The leader has a broader expanse and exposure from which to learn.

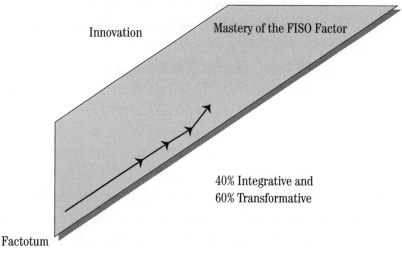

Figure 7-1   The Catalytic Spectrum for Learning

ADOPT AND ADAPT

A business professional needs to adopt an attitude of lifelong learning in order to adapt to an ever-changing business culture. Business cultures change as a result of changes in market conditions and management and from a myriad of other social, economic, and political stimuli. When you encounter a new workforce, either by taking a new job or going to a new company, first watch and learn. You may adopt some of the overt behaviors, but keep your eyes open as to how and why you might make improvements that reflect the perspectives you bring to this environment.

Adopt

Lifelong learning depends on adopting an interest in knowledge— becoming a dedicated seeker of knowledge. This requires forethought, especially for C-level leaders, who are subject to several unique barriers to learning. First, there is the barrier of infallibility. This occurs when leaders are presumed by others to be all knowing and without need of new knowledge. (Sometimes leaders, particularly when they have been very successful, make the fatal mistake of believing in their own infallibility.) Second, there is the barrier of position. Because of their place at the top of the corporate hierarchy, the information that leaders receive is often repeatedly interpreted and revised before it ever reaches their ears. As a result of these filters, important trends and potential clues to solving dilemmas and addressing the needs of the marketplace can be muffled or lost entirely. Worse, because of a leader's power, subordinates often purposely twist information to protect or further their own careers.

A surprising number of CEOs and corporate officers are motivated by more than stature and money. They know that "protecting" their job does not payoff. The objective of a successful enterprise and ultimately a successful, productive, and meaningful career is to contribute to the solution and make a difference.

Some individuals may know this and be quite good performers, but then stop learning and start protecting their jobs. One of the premier research studies on why once-talented individuals in a business organization derail has been done by the Center for Creative Leadership, which has worked with a multitude of different people, functions, and industries over the last several decades. Of the ten fatal flaws their research reveals, the majority of them have one thing in common—the employee has stopped adopting and adapting. The ten fatal flaws can be summarized as follows:

1. Specific performance problems with the business
2. Insensitivity to others: an abrasive, intimidating, bullying style
3. Cold, aloof, arrogant
4. Betrayal of trust
5. Overmanaging: failing to delegate or build a team
6. Overly ambitious: thinking of the next job, playing politics
7. Failing to staff effectively
8. Inability to think strategically
9. Unable to adapt to a boss with a different style
10. Overdependence on a mentor or advocate

FISO Factor leaders must become knowledge seekers in order to overcome these barriers to learning. They must seek out learning as well as become astute questioners and effective listeners.

Tap the Sources of Learning

I make it a policy never to miss an opportunity to learn from an expert. So, in 2001, when Peter Drucker asked for questions at the end of his speech, I was on my feet in a flash. I asked him what was the single most important thing to which leaders should pay attention. The answer was short, swift, and unexpected. "Demographics," said Drucker.

There is a lot of knowledge packed into that word. Demographics measure and describe the characteristics of human populations. They can tell you, for instance, the size and composition of your labor pool and the economic movements in the marketplace. Demographic trends suggest what the future has in store for you. When you know that the birth and death rates in the United States are declining, you know that the older segments of the population are growing at a rate disproportionate to the younger segments. This, of course, has tremendous implications for all companies.

The study of demographics represents only one of many sources of learning into which the FISO Factor leader can tap. We can learn through formal education, through reading, through direct observation, and through the many people we meet and interact with throughout our lives. Anything that can produce an "aha!" moment inside our minds is a source of learning. I recently heard Howard Schultz, the chairman of Starbucks Coffee Company, speak on the subject of healthcare. Starbucks has been much praised for extending healthcare benefits to part-time workers, but Schultz says the company is confronting a nationwide crisis. How does he know this? In the next two years, Starbucks will spend more on healthcare than it does on coffee. This fact shocked me into a greater awareness and stimulated my thinking.

A simple piece of data can also alert us to opportunity. Jeff Bezos started Amazon.com after reading that Internet usage was growing at 2300 percent per *month*. Statisticians talk about "outliers"—data points that fall outside the range. Outliers are often discarded, treated like unimportant anomalies, and ignored. However, they sometimes hide valuable opportunities. How did Howard Schultz discover Starbucks? He was selling kitchen equipment for a Swedish company, when he noticed that a company in Seattle was buying a surprising number of espresso machines. How did Ray Kroc discover McDonalds? He was selling milkshake machines and became curious about a restaurant that ordered eight at one time.

Ask Astute Questions

"A prudent question is one-half of wisdom," said Francis Bacon, the English philosopher who first proposed the inductive method of scientific knowledge. Questions are two-edged swords. A poorly phrased question can shut down the flow of knowledge in an instant, but an astute question can open the door to tremendous learning. The secret of astute questioners is their clear understanding of when to ask open-ended questions and how to continue their questioning to develop a dialogue.

Aspiring leaders should always be asking more than telling. Leaders often think their job is to tell, but, in reality, one good question can accomplish more than telling until you are hoarse. Jeff Thull, president of The Prime Resource Group, teaches this lesson to professional salespeople. Thull finds that sales presentations are largely a waste of time. Instead of telling customers what they need, salespeople should be asking them about their problems. Toward that end, he says salespeople should act more like doctors. Good doctors do not prescribe treatments until they conduct a thorough diagnosis. A fundamental part of that diagnosis is questioning the patient. Leaders, too, can be more effective if they question before they prescribe.

There are times when a "why" question forces a person to rationalize and make up an answer. However, in a nonthreatening environment, a why question is appropriate. Cathy Higgins, one of my firm's affiliates and managing partner of Higgins Kreischer & Associates, identifies two kinds of questions—"why" questions and "why not" questions. Why questions, says Cathy, cultivate analytical thinking and are especially suited to incremental improvements in results. Toyota, for instance invented a technique called the *five whys*, in which the root cause of problems is discovered by repeatedly asking why. Why not questions, says Cathy, promote original thinking and encourage us to reach for breakthrough innovation. In 1961, John F. Kennedy asked why not go to the moon and, in doing so, set in motion what Neil Armstrong called "mankind's giant step."

How you ask questions will determine how successful you will be in receiving a full range of possibilities and ultimately a meaningful recommendation or point of view. Leaders can inadvertently staunch the flow of information if they ask questions that imply blame or hint at accusation. There is no worse way to attempt to solve a problem than asking, "What did you do wrong?" Likewise, leaders often make the mistake of posing questions that telegraph the answer they want to hear. Ask a leading question such as, "You didn't do that, did you?" and chances are very good that you will hear exactly the answer you asked for, whether or not it is exactly accurate. Finally, you can constrict the flow of information by asking questions too quickly. Give people a chance to answer and then, ask more questions based on their answers. Sometimes, as Toyota learned long ago, you need to drill a little deeper to get to the most meaningful answers.

Listen!

It is amazing how clearly things appear to us in hindsight. The value of overnight package delivery now seems obvious, but Fred Smith received a "C" when he proposed it in a college paper. The hapless professor wrote, "…in order to earn better than a 'C,' the idea must be feasible." If great ideas are so obvious why do so few people have them? The most common reason is that they are not listening. There is a lot of truth in the old saw that goes: God gave us one mouth and two ears because he wanted us to listen twice as much as we talk. Even the best questions can only surface information. It is up to you to hear the answers and that is why listening skills are such a critical part of learning.

Effective listening is neutral listening. I learned this during my first project review as a young CPA at Arthur Andersen. I wanted to be the best new hire the firm had ever had, and in my mind my entire future was riding on this performance evaluation. After an early assignment and during the performance evaluation, the first thing my boss said was that my handwriting was terrible and unless it improved, it would hold me back. It seems silly now, but I was devastated. To this day, I cannot remember anything else he said. As it turned out, it was a small price to pay for a valuable lesson: You need to disengage emotionally as you listen, even when you are being told things you do not want to hear. Otherwise, your emotions can easily get in the way of what you should be hearing.

Effective listening is also wholehearted listening. As any Zen Buddhist can tell you, it is difficult to stay in the moment. Our minds wander or we get fixated on one piece of information. The problem is the moment we stop listening, we stop learning. Fifteen years ago, Bob McVicker, my boss at Kraft Food's R&D Technology Center, gave me a fine piece advice: "Be aware of when you stopped listening," he said. "As soon as you think of something else, draw a line in your mind. If that line appears before the person has stopped talking, you aren't listening well."

Effective listening is active listening. Listening is not a solitary act. When you listen, you are also communicating. You are telling the speaker how you perceive him through your actions and attitudes. Here are a few tips I have used to become an active listener:

- Minimize distractions. Do not try to do two things at once. When talking to others, do not take phone calls or check your e-mail. Focus your attention on the speaker.
- Make eye contact. Eye contact shows speakers that you are interested in what they have to say.
- Demonstrate your interest. A simple nod or a short phrase, such as "I see," tells speakers that you are hearing them.
- Confirm your understanding. When the speaker is finished, do not respond before confirming that you understood what they have told you by paraphrasing their main points.
- Pay attention to nonverbal signals. A frown can signal disagreement or confusion; a smile can signal disrespect to the speaker or

the message. Let your expression and other actions reflect the message.

Remember, effective listening is continual listening. The business world, like the rest of the universe, is a dynamic environment. It is always changing, and thus the answers that we hear will always be changing too. If we do not listen continually, we can easily miss messages that are critical for our success and survival.

FOUR LEARNING SKILLS

When Harvard Business School professor David Garvin studied learning initiatives, he found that successful organizational strategies are situational—they vary with the challenges faced by individual organizations. However, he did find one important commonality: A leader who values learning will strive to create an organization that values teaching and learning. Further, he found that leaders who are effective learners exhibit four traits:

- They are open to new perspectives. FISO Factor leaders accept the fact that change is the only constant. They recognize that they must continually challenge established "truths" and revise those beliefs whenever their validity fails.
- They recognize their internal biases. FISO Factor leaders understand that everyone thinks and learns differently. They ensure that personal and organization blind spots do not cause them to miss important learning opportunities.
- They seek unfiltered data. FISO Factor leaders know that as information moves through the organization, it

undergoes a filtering process that can change its meaning. To avoid this, they go directly to the source of information whenever possible.

• They maintain a sense of humility. FISO Factor leaders recognize that they do not have all the answers. They understand the limits of their own knowledge and relentlessly seek out the best answers no matter where those answers reside.

Adapt

Once you have adopted the attitude of lifelong learning and been exposed to acceptable attitudes and behaviors that have worked well in the past environment, the transformation of the data into useful knowledge begins. This work is accomplished through a process of adaptation. It requires that you reflect and connect information to create useful implications that lead to added-value behavior and improved results.

Reflect

One of the common misconceptions regarding great leaders is that they are instantaneous decision makers. In fact, it is often a mistake to charge into action as soon as you finish gathering information. Take the time to reflect and test the validity of what you have heard. Deliberative, thoughtful action is a mark of wisdom.

Starbucks' Howard Schultz likes to tell the story of how he tried to kill the idea for Frappuccino. A store manager in Los Angeles invented the drink, but Schultz did not want to make the substantial investment in blenders and ice equipment needed to mix the new concoction. Luckily, the manager decided to test market the product in her own store. As the lines of customers continued to request this new product, the results of the test convinced Schultz to invest and roll out this offering throughout the system. Today, bottled Frappuccino is a $500 million business and Starbucks stores also mix and sell hundreds of millions of dollars worth of the drink. Schultz calls it "the best idea I ever said 'no' to."

So, take some time to think about the information you gather. Consider the advice of Stanford University professor Roderick Kramer. Kramer studied the symptoms of reckless leadership and found: "Many leaders' misdeeds begin as snap decisions made in the course of their normal, busy days. The decisions may seem inconsequential or easy to delegate to subordinates or aides. But once made, they take on a life of their own." How can you avoid this trap? Ask yourself, says Kramer, "Is this a good time to pause, consider doing something different, or even do nothing at all?"

Connect

The next issue in the process of adapting information is the establishment of the connection between what you have learned and your current situation. Aspiring leaders are always asking, How can I use this information to improve my personal performance and my company's performance?

Keith Alm, a former colleague at Sara Lee, who went on to become CEO of Hallmark International, Inc., a division of greeting card giant Hallmark Cards, was a wonderful model for this connective drive. Keith is a seeker of knowledge—he kept himself informed by reading a wide variety of books and periodicals. He is also a sharp-eyed observer of the world, who when I worked with him, was constantly jotting notes throughout the day and after market visits, following up on many of the ideas generated.

It was Keith who convinced Sara Lee's senior management team to expand into Asia. The company was focused on Eastern and Central Europe, but when Keith traveled through Asia in the early nineties, what he saw convinced him of the markets' potential. He came back and described what he had seen—the great masses of people and their energy, construction projects running 24/7, and the tremendous manufacturing power of the region. He connected what he saw to the company's need for ever-more-efficient production and ever-larger markets.

Keith also helped pioneer the mass production of printed T-shirts. At that time, printed T-shirts were made in small batches in print shops. Sara Lee, like other large manufacturers, only made blank shirts, which they sold to the print shops. Then, Keith went on vacation to Southern California and came across T-shirts made by a small company named Hang Ten. Hang Ten was manufacturing printed T-shirts and selling them at a handsome margin. He brought the idea back home, licensed the rights to print the logos of sports teams, and quickly established a lucrative new business for Sara Lee.

There are legions of stories like this in business. The idea for Velcro, for instance, was inspired by a burr. The overhead trolleys that moved beef in the meat packing industry inspired Henry Ford's assembly line. The important lesson in each is to make the connection—to synthesize "what you have learned" into "what you can do next."

APPLY LEARNING WITH THE FIVE A'S

FISO Factor leaders are savvy change agents. They know that, in business, companies learn in order to grow, and that growth is always accomplished through a process of change. That is why the final leg in the learning journey encompasses the successful application of information and knowledge through change management.

The hard reality is that change in a business environment is almost always a group effort. Even the most accomplished leaders cannot accomplish organizational change alone. Instead, they must act as agents of change and depend on others to execute their learning.

There are many noteworthy change process texts and models. At the LIF Group, we use a process model that has evolved through the study of best practices and practical experience. We call it the five A's: *awareness, anecdote, alignment, action,* and *achievement*. All five steps comprise the financial focus process to improve profitable growth.

In the awareness stage, leaders break the "conspiracy of silence." Too often, no one wants to acknowledge the problems and opportunities that the change is designed to address. The organization may be deaf to the problems. The old children's tale about the emperor who has no clothes applies. Often, no one wants to tell the boss what is wrong and assumes silence is a safer gamut. Change agents shine a spotlight on the issue and direct the attention of the organization toward it. They force the organization to recognize the factual situation and trends.

In the anecdote stage, leaders inspire and motivate their constituents to undertake change. This is often accomplished through the telling of powerful stories. These might be stories that reach back into the corporate history or portraits of the positive future that waits when the change is accomplished (or the negative future that awaits if the change is resisted).

In the alignment stage, leaders ensure that all of the resources required to create successful change are present and synchronized. These resources include the allocation of tangible elements, such as funding and materials. They also encompass the many intangible elements that often spell the difference between failure and success in change efforts. These can include the knowledge and training that employees need to undertake the change and the cultural alterations that might be necessary to support the change. This also means the alignment of processes, performance measurement systems, and reward plans.

In the action stage, execution is the order of the day. This is where the "rubber meets the road." Leaders now act as frontline generals, who direct and redirect the action as unanticipated circumstances arise, and, as is almost always the case, the shortcomings of the change plan are revealed. Timely revisions and a daily commitment to address new circumstances through corrective or preventative action are hallmarks of this stage.

Finally, in the achievement stage, the results of the effort are measured and feedback is gathered. The continual process of improvement begins. The learning that has been implemented is refined and generates new learning. The FISO leader implements the new learning and continues the process of growth.

I know that this brief description of the five A's makes change efforts sound fairly straightforward and easily accomplished. (Visit www.FISOFactor.com for more information.) The truth, however, is that no matter how adroit a leader is at managing change, there are always bumps in the road. So, I would like to offer several supplementary lessons that might help you avoid or overcome some of the barriers to successful change efforts that I have encountered.

Perfection Is the Enemy of Progress

Learning requires change, but it does not require perfection. Too often, leaders and organizations stall because they believe they must become experts before they undertake change. They pursue detailed knowledge and educate everyone in the company, while their opportunities pass them by.

I worked for BIC in France for three years, but I am sure there are many people who would look down their noses at my limited ability to speak French. When I took the job, I quickly learned the basics of the language and jumped into work. In speaking the language in day-to-day life and making many mistakes, I learned more than I could have in months of classes. I also gained a working knowledge of the language as opposed to an academic knowledge. Perfect French, as it turned out, was not a necessity. The company's executives came from a variety of nations and English was used far more often than I had supposed it would be. (Looking back, I realize that it was a question of establishing priorities. My priority was to learn how to improve BIC's financial position and management, not speak flawless French.)

Past Performance Can Provide Future Knowledge

Past performance does not guarantee future results, but it surely provides a valuable source of learning. That is why making the time to review the results of past actions and projects is an important task.

Successful leaders evaluate and learn from their own performance. Peter Drucker, for instance, has conducted personal reviews since the early 1940s. He says, "I have set aside two weeks every summer in which to review my work during the preceding year, beginning with the things that I did poorly and the things I should have done but did not do."

Successful leaders also review organizational performance. When I was responsible for worldwide planning at Kraft Foods, I conducted such a review with the division planners after our first budget cycle. We established what had and had not worked well in the process and as a result, changed the schedule so we could complete the company's 120 departmental budgets in August instead of November. In this way, the department heads were able to focus on generating revenue instead of planning during the perennially busy final quarter. The change paid additional dividends when Philip Morris made its bid to acquire Kraft. Because we had the next year's budgets already in hand, we were able to knowledgeably respond to Philip Morris's offer and maximize the purchase price for Kraft shareholders.

Failure Is Inevitable, but Large Losses Are Not

By this time, every leader knows that failures in business are inevitable and understands that failures also offer a valuable source of learning. There is the classic story of IBM's Thomas Watson, Sr., who refused to accept the resignation of a junior executive whose mistake cost the company $10 million. "You can't be serious," Watson purportedly said, "We just spent $10 million educating you."

Watson's intention was laudable, but was it financially sound? Failures may be inevitable but they do not have to be expensive. Companies use test marketing and pilot projects to gain experience and limit their losses. Aspiring leaders should also be thinking about how to limit the cost of failure in their careers.

Early in my career, I volunteered to start the Kellogg Graduate School of Management's alumni club in Chicago and served as its program chair for a couple of years. The position required that I recruit a team of volunteers, organize ten events per year, and convince prominent people to speak without payment. I made mistakes and learned a multitude of valuable lessons about leading teams, reaching and dealing with influential and powerful people, and ensuring the success of meetings and other events. Even better, because I learned these lessons outside work, the cost of my mistakes was minimal and did not negatively affect my career at all.

SAWHANEY ON LEARNING

Dr. Mohanbir Sawhney is the Director of the Kellogg School of Management's Center for Research in Technology and Innovation and cofounder of the Kellogg Innovation Network. Here is his advice for developing the FISO Factor catalyst of learning:

- *Practice intellectual arbitrage.* Earn a profit by transplanting ideas. Cast a wide net for ideas and inventions that work in other industries and disciplines, but have not yet been discovered by your competitors.

- *Don't get locked into paradigms.* Always keep an open mind. If you are locked into the "zero-sum" concept of competitive strategy, for example, you won't be able to see the possibilities of collaboration.
- *Immerse yourself in data.* The more "dots" you have, the easier it is to connect them to see the big picture. And don't forget to pay special attention to aberrations in the data.
- *Don't try to force data into your model.* The most common barrier to effective learning is the human tendency to twist facts to fit their assumptions.

CREATE A LEARNING ORGANIZATION

The concept of the learning organization has received a great deal of attention since Peter Senge's *The Fifth Discipline* was first published in 1990. In it, Senge quoted Arie de Geus, then director of Shell International, who declared, "The ability to learn faster than your competition may be the only sustainable competitive advantage."

You do not have to take de Geus's word for this. Recently, a firm named Bassi Investments created portfolios based on the stocks of companies that make large investments in employee education and development. One portfolio, which was launched in 2001, returned 36.2 percent, 8 percent more than the S&P 500 through November 3, 2004. The other, which was launched in 2003, returned 41.4 percent compared to a 34.5 percent return on the S&P 500. This led Laurie Bassi, the firm's CEO and chairman, to conclude that even though employee education is classified as an expense in financial reporting, it is better thought of as an investment. Simply put, organizational learning pays. And, that is why FISO Factors leaders try to implant and develop the catalytic agent of learning throughout their companies.

One effective way to spread learning and generate knowledge is to encourage all employees to question the status quo. Arte Nathan, who is something of a human resources legend in the gaming industry and currently chief human resource officer of Wynn Resorts, is a committed devotee of this strategy. He says:

> Every day, every week I challenge my staff not to do things because we've always done them, but to look at what needs to be done. We have a rule around here in that we always have to ask why, no matter what we do. If we have a program, why should we do it? If we have a policy, what's the reason for it? If we give an instruction to someone, they have the right to ask why. And we must be able to explain it. That creates a mindset that you're always re-examining things. You are always trying to understand that underlying basis of whatever it is you're trying to do. If you practice that on a continual basis, it has the tendency to clear out the plaque. It's too easy to fall into complacency.

Another strategy to encourage organizational learning is to create formal and informal communication pathways that are dedicated to knowledge capture and retention. As we said in Chapter 6, leaders tend to underestimate the knowledge inherent in the workforce. When consultants could not produce compelling ideas for new magazines, Mary Berner, president and CEO of Fairchild Publications, solicited editorial concepts from her employees. "We [heard from] a 19-year-old assistant in the circulation department who is putting herself through college," she said, "along with a marketing manager and a magazine editor in chief—and we were all impressed and surprised by their knowledge and the quality of their ideas." In fact, four employee-originated concepts are now in development.

At Hannaford Bros. Co., we created formal "learning groups" to stimulate the acquisition and transfer of knowledge. These groups were cross-functional, bringing together associates from different departments and functional areas. They would work on specific issues, problems, or opportunities. They would also stay together for long periods, forming a "web" to spread learning to various parts of the organization.

Finally, it also makes good sense to extend the organization's learning reach beyond corporate boundaries. Recently, Steve Ballmer did this at Microsoft by creating a buddy program in which employees are formally paired with independent software developers. The Microsoft employees are charged with making it easier for independent developers to work with the software giant, as well as making sure that the company learns what it can from the developers. "We need to make it business as usual to listen to the voices of customers and partners," Ballmer told employees in the e-mail announcing the program.

There are many more ways to encourage organizational learning—scenario planning, corporate universities, sabbaticals, tuition benefits, community and philanthropic volunteer programs, to name a few. The list is limited only by your imagination and budget. The salient point here is that successful leaders are deeply committed to organizational learning, as well as personal learning.

LEARNING YIELDS INNOVATION

Just as the language of business includes the discussion of cash statements, with its sources and uses of funds, in learning we can also distinguish between sources and uses of knowledge. We have already discussed the sources of knowledge. Now, we can define its uses. In business, learning is not an end in and of itself. It is an investment and like any investment, its aim is to produce a profit. The profit that is derived from the catalytic agent of learning comes in the form of *innovation*.

The application of learning to the process of fitting-in provides the basis for practical innovation. You must learn "what is" before you can reach for "what could be." Take the example of Michael Armstrong at the beginning of his tenure as AT&T's CEO. When Armstrong held his first press conference as CEO, the media pressed him to divulge his plans for transforming the venerable, and vulnerable, company. Armstrong replied that his first task would be to *listen*. "Paradoxically," explains Dick Martin, AT&T's former head of media relations, "the best way for the CEO to engage employees initially is not to give a rousing speech, but to listen." Actually, it is not such a paradox. The leader who does not bother to learn what is happening within his company and within the minds and hearts of its employees cannot hope to create feasible futures. Further, as we have already seen, if you cannot fit in, you cannot lead the change efforts that are necessary to successfully innovate.

Learning itself is the process by which leaders produce the knowledge needed to create innovation, transform their companies, *and* stand out. For instance, when newly appointed CEO Emanuel Kampouris set out to rebuild American Standard's business model in order to improve its financial results, "he literally traveled the world in search of tools and techniques that would help his company." One of the tools he discovered was DFM (demand flow manufacturing), which is based on the tenets of lean manufacturing and the concept that customer demand should drive production. Kampouris implemented DFM throughout American Standard and tripled Standard's inventory turns. The enhanced efficiency added $460 million annually to the company's bottom line.

The catalytic agent of learning is a never-ending source of career and organizational advantage. It has the power to release the leader within you and the leadership potential of your company. The ability to learn is like a muscle: the more you use it, the stronger it becomes. The more you exercise the muscle of learning, the more useful you become to your company. The more useful you become, the faster your career progresses.

THE ABCS OF LEARNING

Here are some thought-starter questions for learning.

Fitting In with Learning

Attitude: Be open-minded. What internal prejudices stifle your ability to learn? How can you modify your behavior to attract more knowledge?

Behavior: Tap into the corporate knowledge base. Where does the "corporate memory" reside in your company? What learning resources already exist and how can you utilize them?

Characteristic: Learn from the past. Can you conduct regular performance reviews? How can you turn yesterday's mistakes into tomorrow's successes?

Standing Out with Learning

Attitude: Challenge the "scared cows." What are the assumptions in your business model? How can you alter them to improve your results?

Behavior: Cast a wide net for information. What books and periodicals can you read that cover subjects outside your industry and profession? What volunteer opportunities can you undertake to acquire new skills?

Characteristic: Say "yes." How can you encourage the acquisition and adoption of new information? In what ways can you adapt and apply new learning while simultaneously limiting risk?

8

PERSPECTIVE: THE
PRISM OF INSIGHT

In the summer of 1664, Isaac Newton purchased a prism at the Stourbridge Fair, held annually on the outskirts of Cambridge, and began a series of experiments that changed our understanding of the nature of light. Until that time, those who studied "natural philosophy" believed that a prism somehow created the colors that became visible when light passed through it. Newton, however, proved that the range of color a prism produces is inherent in the light. By bending the path of the white light, a prism separates its colors and makes them visible. White light, declared the famous philosopher and alchemist, is actually composed of a spectrum of colors.

Just as light is composed of a spectrum of colors, a FISO Factor leader's decisions are composed of a spectrum of perspectives. The best leadership decisions have the clarity of white light, but if you could view them through a prism, you would see that many of them are actually composed of a range of perspectives. Witness The Pepsi Bottling Group (PBG) and the meltdown of the Russian economy in 1998.

PBG, the $11 billion manufacturer and distributor of Pepsi brands, had recently assumed responsibility for the soft drink giant's Russian business when that country's economy collapsed. The ruble collapsed, dropping overnight from 7 to the U.S. dollar to 22 to the dollar. Inflation exploded and Russian consumers, many of whom had lost virtually all their savings, stopped spending. Pepsi sales plummeted 60 percent and PBG's Russian business was losing $100 million on an annualized basis.

John Cahill, who is now PBG's CEO, but at the time was CFO with responsibility for international operations, remembers, "Business as usual was not an option. In addition to the pressure of the losses, we had the company's IPO in the planning stage. We had mostly expatriates running the business and my own knowledge of Russia was limited. So, reaching out for perspectives was a necessity."

First, John reached out for internal perspectives. He discussed possible strategies with PBG CEO Craig Weatherup, who created the business model that gave Pepsi greater focus and energy by splitting the company's brand management from its bottling and distribution operations. He also reached out to Roger Enrico, parent company PepsiCo's notable brand builder and CEO. Their perspectives led John to the conclusion that cost cutting alone could not solve the dilemma in Russia. In fact, reducing the price of Pepsi in Russia could well endanger the value of the brand itself. Instead, with the support of Weatherup and Enrico, John chose to develop and introduce a less expensive "B brand" named Fiesta in the Russian market. This ran counter to Pepsi's heritage of pursuing only premium brands. But, it enabled PBG to protect the value of the Pepsi brand while maintaining the company's Russian customer base.

John also reached out for external perspectives. The existing company team in Russia was charged with implanting the Pepsi culture and processes in that country. Now, the team required a new perspective. It had to change the way it did business to reflect the unique needs of its national market, as well as to market and sell an unfamiliar, inexpensive product. So, John rebuilt the Russian team using local executives and managers. They understood the market in a way that few outsiders could and were less resistant to a B-brand strategy.

"Most of the insights came from our own reorganized team," recalls John. "We spent a lot of time together, setting a course for affordable growth, controlling pricing, cutting out most of the cost structure, and rearchitecting the distribution system." The strategy, which John created with the help of internal and external perspectives, enabled PBG to turn its Russian business around. After the crisis, the business quickly returned to profitability, and PBG has since multiplied its product offerings fivefold and increased volume at double-digit rates annually.

As John Cahill's example shows, informed and shared perspectives can help leaders to solve difficult problems and create viable strategies for growing their businesses. Thoughtful and practical perspectives, particularly those of key constituencies, are also critical in the successful execution of these strategies. An aspiring leader cannot hope to enlist the support of stakeholders unless she can present her plans in ways that are aligned with their interests. Understanding stakeholders' perspectives is an important step toward identifying those interests.

For these reasons and more, the fifth catalytic agent of the FISO Factor is perspective. The catalyst of perspective helps leaders fit in. It provides insight into the views, demands, and needs of internal stakeholders, such as employees, superiors, and boards of directors. This enables an aspiring leader to align his perspective with the organizational culture. Perspective also helps leaders stand out. The source of an external perspective can be former competitors or employees of other companies, a trade group or association, or even different industry experiences that may have approached similar but radically different specific dilemmas. It enables leaders to stand in the shoes of external stakeholders, such as investors, customers, and suppliers, and

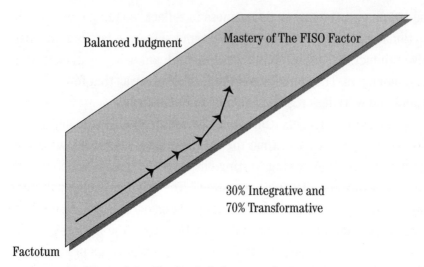

Balanced Judgment

Mastery of The FISO Factor

30% Integrative and
70% Transformative

Factotum

Figure 8-1   The Catalytic Spectrum for Perspectives

bring their expectations, demands, and attitudes to the corporate table. The insights gained from these external perspectives allow aspiring leaders to begin transforming their companies, the most productive use of the catalyst of perspective, as illustrated in Figure 8-1.

THE LEADER'S PERSPECTIVE

Around 600 B.C., Greek stone carvers inscribed the words "know thyself" at the Delphic Oracle on Mount Parnassus. This ancient command is particularly appropriate for today's leaders. As we saw in the last chapter, C-level leaders can become isolated from the daily realities of business because their positions of authority and power remove them from functional decision making. Because of the acclaim that often accompanies success, they can also begin to believe in their own infallibility. When these situations occur, leaders can lose their sense of perspective.

The loss of perspective causes leaders to do and say things that can cost them dearly. Hotelier Leona Helmsley is one such case. She is currently the 274th richest person in the world, according to *Forbes*, but she is just as well known for saying, "We don't pay taxes. Only the little people pay taxes." Helmsley was convicted of tax evasion in 1989, fined $7.1 million, and sentenced to four years in jail. She served 18 months of the sentence in a federal penitentiary. Why did she evade $1.7 million in taxes when she was worth more than 20 times that amount? The prosecutor claimed it was greed, but it appears that Helmsley had lost her sense of perspective long before.

The problem with losing your perspective is that you can miss things that should be blindingly obvious. The Martha Stewart case provides another high-profile example. Stewart, a highly successful entrepreneur and a billionaire, incurred over $3 million in legal fees, served a prison sentence, and endangered the survival of the company she founded because of an insider trading charge valued at $51,000. Interestingly, Stewart appears to have become resigned to her defeat and regained her perspective *after* the verdict. She chose to serve her sentence and get on with her life and career rather than wait out the appeals process.

The two examples above both involve women, but there is no gender line when it comes to perspective. We are all vulnerable to this trap. Further, our own mental processes conspire to conceal our flaws. It is very difficult to "know yourself" by simply looking at your reflection in a mirror.

William H. Macy, the actor and screenwriter who cocreated and starred in a movie titled "Door to Door," illuminated this point during a television interview. The inspirational film tells the true story of Bill Porter, a man with cerebral palsy who refused to allow others to limit his opportunities and became the most successful salesman at the Whitman Company, a direct marketer of household goods. The role led Macy to become a spokesperson and a trustee for United Cerebral Palsy. It also made him keenly aware of prejudice and the ways in which our perspectives can become warped. Had Porter allowed others' perspectives of him to determine his aspirations or potential, he would never have accomplished what he did. Limited perspectives are often times a root cause of prejudice. "You learn a bit about the nature of prejudice," said Macy of his experience, "It rears its head in unexpected ways. It catches all of us. It is very hard to guard against it. . . . It creeps in."

Developing and maintaining a broad perspective can defend one against prejudice, parochialism, and other diseases that depend on a limited world view. So, how can you keep yourself firmly grounded, guard against destructive mental patterns, and maintain a realistic perspective? The answer lies in looking outside yourself. Perhaps the best places to look are in literature, works of philosophy and history, and the friends and business contacts you have.

Business is but one aspect of life's experience, hardly distinct or isolated from the environment in which it functions. Business success depends upon people, and therefore upon awareness of politics, social trends, attitudes and values, and a myriad of other expressions of human emotions, fears, drives, and desires. Literature and philosophy are the best sources for appreciating whatever universals might exist among people over time and place. Literature and history allow for a more time sensitive and culturally determined appreciation of the human condition. One example that resounds with me is from the U.S. civil rights leader Dr. Martin Luther King, Jr., and his "Letter from the Birmingham City Jail," which he wrote in response to a public statement directed at him by eight Alabama clergymen on April 12, 1963. In Dr. King's response, he rebutted the "outsiders coming in" and masterfully explained that people want to be part of the system. He wrote that the outsiders are knocking on the door, but want to do it by their rules and in their time.

Business cannot hope to prosper in a foreign country, be it Romania, China, or Peru, without an appreciation for the values, beliefs, social mores, politics, tastes, and fears of the people in that country. Philosophy, history, and literature can provide the access to thoughts and feelings of a culture—and in the process develop a broader perspective in the reader. We will discuss the broader global citizenship catalytic agent and developing this skill in Chapter 9.

GAINING OTHER PEOPLE'S PERSPECTIVES

FISO Factor leaders know that everything does not revolve around them. They do *not* have a leader-centric view of the world. Instead, they embrace a multicentric view. In this view, there are many centers of power, all of which exert influence. A leader is only one node in this more dynamic and realistic network view of business. She is part of a larger system—a business unit, a company, a culture, an industry, a world—within which there are many perspectives.

The core competency of the catalytic agent of perspective is the ability to elicit and incorporate the relevant and influential perspectives into strategies for growth and change. When aspiring leaders master this competence—the ability to assimilate and have moments of true insight and, even times, conversion—they enhance their decision-making processes and unleash their ability to successfully execute their plans and strategies. There are three practices that enable us to unleash the power of this catalyst: the ability to empathize with others, the ability to draw out others and pull in their perspectives, and the ability to create consensus from various perspectives.

Empathize to Identify Perspective

Empathy is the personality trait that enables you to understand other people's situations, feelings, and motives from their perspectives, instead of our own. This is a valuable tool in the learning process. This understanding also allows you to predict the response you will receive to new ideas. You can become more effective at prioritizing, planning, and implementing by thinking like the CEO, the board of directors, employees, customers, and others. These various points of view operate like a reverse prism that bends the spectrum of colors into a clear light or, to follow the simile, an "enlightened" sense of direction.

The degree to which empathy is lacking in business is always surprising to me. It sometimes seems as if everyone only knows and cares about one side of the story. Think about how often employees in the field complain about corporate headquarters. They call it the "puzzle palace" and the "big house," as in a jail. Conversely, those in corporate headquarters often have a correspondingly low opinion of those in the field. Thus, instead of learning from each other's perspectives, they make decisions and take action based on only one side of the story—their own. The results are usually less than perfect.

Maintaining an empathetic connection to the perspectives of others need not be difficult. Even small things can help you shift perspective. Consider Harry Kraemer, the former CEO and chairman of medical products manufacturer Baxter International, Inc., and an employee of the company for more than 20 years. When he was CEO, Kraemer walked by the cubicle in which he had worked when he first joined the company on a daily basis. "I try to remember how I thought when I was sitting in that cube," he explains. "When I make a decision, I try to put myself in the mindset of the person I was 21 years ago. My job is all about taking other perspectives into account." By staying in touch with his roots, Kraemer tries to be attuned to the perspectives of his company's employees.

FISO Factor leaders often go to great lengths to stay in touch with internal and external perspectives. Joe Forehand, formerly CEO and now the chairman of Accenture, is a master of the catalyst of perspective. When Joe started working at the consulting firm 30 years ago, there were 1,000 employees, now there are over 100,000. You might think that leading this vast operation keeps Joe in his office, but he is actually traveling most of time. He recently told me that he visits clients and company employees approximately 200 days per year. What is he doing? He is searching the world for the perspectives on which the firm depends and gathering the insights that those perspectives offer.

"I look to others quite frequently for advice and counsel," says Joe. "I turn to other leaders at Accenture and have always tried, in fact, to build a team of people who do not think as I do. Other key people I turn to include our clients to keep us client-driven . . . our younger people who stimulate new ways of doing things . . . my wife who has an uncanny ability to read people . . . our board and other business leaders to gain a perspective that is from outside Accenture, since I have spent 32 years at one company."

The effort a leader expends in his search for perspectives is a good signal of his willingness to empathize with others. Andrea Redmond, cohead of the CEO/board services practice at executive recruiter Russell Reynolds Associates, defines this willingness as "having heart." She says, "Having heart isn't giving speeches and being involved in not-for-profits. Having heart means being aware of what it's like to stand in somebody else's shoes instead of being so insulated. . . . Nobody wants an insular chief executive anymore."

DO YOU KNOW HOW YOUR BOSS SEES YOU?

Your boss's perceptions of you are among the most important perspectives in your career. This is the perspective that determines the assignments you receive, your compensation, and your promotions. Nevertheless, far too many employees pay it little or no mind. They dutifully sit through annual and semiannual performance reviews—reviews that are often rote and formulaic—with little or no question.

I have never been content with the standard performance review, and when I became CFO at Hannaford Bros., I found that CEO Hugh Farrington felt the same way. When *CFO Magazine* interviewed us for a story on performance reviews, Hugh recalled some of the reviews he had received during his career and said, "You come out of a session like that saying, 'I'll never treat anyone like that.'" Instead, Hugh tried to conduct form-free reviews that were designed to match the personality and needs of the individual. In my case, that meant answering a lot of questions from me. My questions were designed to elicit Hugh's feedback. I wanted to get a clear picture of his perspective on my past performance and his expectations and hopes for me in the coming year. The interesting thing is that we both characterized the resulting reviews as "fun," a far cry from how most employees and their bosses think of performance reviews.

Your challenge, as an aspiring leader, is to understand your boss's perspective. Make full use of performance reviews and other opportunities to reach out for that view. Identify and confirm your boss's perspective and use the insights that are revealed to better fit in and stand out.

Become a Perspective Magnet

The ability to stand in someone else's shoes does not, in and of itself, guarantee access to other people's perspectives. "Other people" must also willingly and voluntarily share their perspectives with you. You cannot force people to share their perspectives or demand them; they must offer them. FISO Factor leaders are experts at encouraging others to share their perspective.

Becoming a magnet capable of attracting other people's perspectives requires many of the same traits that are used in previous FISO

Factor catalysts. People willingly offer their opinions and emotions to leaders who demonstrate open-mindedness, a broad worldview, and well-honed listening and questioning skills. Leaders must also offer others the opportunity to share their perspectives.

The Hewlett-Packard Company's former CEO and chairman Carly Fiorina is a brilliant and inspirational communicator who is known for her confidence. But these qualities occasionally worked against her. For instance, when she first began meeting HP employees in informal meetings, they were disconcerted by her habit of "having all the answers" and not soliciting their input. Thomas Neff and James Citrin of Spencer Stewart write:

> HP people became concerned that Fiorina was not interested in learning about them, about their products, or about the processes by which the business was carried out. . . . But by not asking questions and by not failing to have some answers, she scared many of the employees.

Scared people, of course, do not openly share their perspectives. Instead, they must be convinced that their leaders want to hear from them. Robert "Bob" Chuck, a longtime friend, is a master at the catalyst of perspective. Gathering the perspectives of various stakeholders has been instrumental in his success as senior VP at the world's largest global environmental engineering consulting firm, CH2M Hill, and previously, as manager-chief engineer of Hawaii's Water Resources agency. His ability to understand perspectives without taking sides also stood him in good stead whenever the political power in the state shifted. Here is how Bob creates a perspective-friendly atmosphere:

> I usually have gathered others in an informal setting—stated the need for action and the objectives, and then, listened to others before presenting my thoughts on the subject. During the course of discussions, I have listened more than commented on

141

a person's input and have encouraged questions from others. I try to make sure everyone has a chance to express his or her opinion in a frank way.

People must believe that they can safely say things that might appear to oppose the majority or the "authority" view without jeopardizing their careers and relationships. Several years ago, I witnessed a fine example of how this is accomplished during an industry conference held in Barcelona. I was invited to join a group of executives from the Coca-Cola Company, including Neville Isdell (who was named CEO and chairman in May 2004). At the time of the conference, Coke had been struggling with the issue of leadership for almost five years. The executives at the table were frustrated and unhappy with the company's second CEO since the death of Roberto Goizueta in late 1997.

An extraordinary conversation ensued. The executives at the table obviously felt that they could confide in Neville, who had just retired. After 30 years, he knew the company as intimately as anyone at the table. As an insider/outsider, the executives related to him and also felt safe in sharing with him. It was not Neville's position alone that made him such a magnet for different perspectives. As I watched and listened, I saw how he absorbed and filtered the negative comments. He was open and receptive. He was never defensive nor did he stick to the "corporate line," but at the same time, he carefully questioned the things that he heard that were at odds with his experience. He had a constructive attitude. He turned the conversation from a gripe session into an opportunity to gain and share insight.

This experience suggests an unusual technique for attracting open viewpoints. When trying to solicit other people's perspectives, disassociate yourself from your position, at least momentarily. Try to imagine how you might behave and react as if you had just retired from your company and were having a heart-to-heart chat with former colleagues who were still in the thick of the action.

Utilize Perspective to Build Consensus

Using the catalyst of perspective as a tool for decision making is only part of its value to the FISO Factor leader. The prism of insight is also a valuable tool for building consensus. As we have already seen, leaders do not create change single-handedly; they must enlist the support of their followers. Leaders build the coalitions necessary to create change and growth by addressing and aligning the various perspectives of their followers. Whether the situation demands consensus, coalition, or authoritarian decision making, absorbing a wide range of perspectives will improve the process and ultimately, the chosen course of action.

This is not to say that a leader must "knuckle under" to all of the demands of differing perspectives. If that were the case, little change would be accomplished. There are always a few people who actively resist change and will not be convinced. It is clear, to paraphrase President Abraham Lincoln, that you cannot please all of the people all of the time. Happily, consensus does not require unanimity.

To build consensus, leaders must acknowledge and consider differing perspectives. Look at how Charles Rossotti approached the gargantuan task of rebuilding the Internal Revenue Service. In 1997, when Rossotti became the first businessperson to serve as commissioner, the IRS had the largest customer base and the lowest approval rating of any American organization. It was under attack from its own employees, taxpayers, tax practitioners, the media, Congress, and even the Clinton administration.

As you might guess, Rossotti quickly discovered that it was impossible to create a strategy that could encompass and reconcile all of these diverse, and conflicting, perspectives. But he also knew that he could not fulfill his mandate to restructure and improve the moribund agency without the support of all of those stakeholders. He says:

> I had to find opportunities to meet with people in settings that encouraged them to get below the surface—to tell me what was

truly on their minds and to solicit their support on fixing the real problems we were facing in trying to change the IRS. It was hard to do this in Washington, where time is chopped into tiny pieces, especially for members of Congress. So I sought opportunities to visit key members in their home districts. It was also important to meet with tax practitioners, business groups, and IRS employees on their own turf and in small groups.

Rossotti did not promise to fulfill every concern of each of these groups. Instead, he listened and acknowledged that he understood their perspectives and their problems. Then, he presented his perspective and his plan to each group. He asked for their help and they gave it. He built a consensus. In June 1998, Congress passed a bill reflecting virtually all of the ideas in his plan to reform the IRS—a plan that called for the greatest degree of change at the agency since 1952. On July 22, President Clinton signed the bill into law.

RECOGNIZING THE SIX PERSPECTIVES ON CHANGE

By identifying the perspectives at work among stakeholders, FISO Factor leaders can more effectively create the consensus needed to successfully undertake innovation and change efforts. Jim Selman, CEO of ParaComm Partners International, offers some insight into these perspectives in his study of the six ways people relate to their circumstances and to change itself:

- *Resisting:* a mindset that "opposes" change by denying that the circumstances compelling change ever exist.
- *Coping:* a mindset that "responds positively" or acknowledges that the circumstances requiring change exist, but maintains that they cannot be overcome.

- *Responding:* a mindset that "owns" the current circumstances and understands the need for new situations, but maintains that the current conditions cannot be changed because of greater external forces.
- *Choosing:* a mindset that "accepts" the circumstances which compel change and the proposed changes.
- *Bringing Forth:* a mindset that actively "creates" circumstances for an acceptable response to new facts and change.
- *Mastery:* a mindset that in addition to creating circumstances that compel and demand change, seeks to influence and create the revised and new "context" within which circumstances and change will thrive.

To build consensus, leaders need to *convince* those stakeholders who are resisting and coping, *encourage* those are responding and choosing, and *embrace* those who are bringing forth change and have the mastery required to alter the very context of the business environment.

CREATING ORGANIZATIONAL PERSPECTIVE

The catalyst of perspective, like each of the FISO Factor catalysts, has valuable organizational applications. As we have seen repeatedly, leaders alone cannot move companies. Thus, they must spread the power of perspective throughout their companies in order to enhance institutional decision making and create more responsive organizations.

In the last ten to fifteen years, this realization has been growing within the corporate community. Businesses are aggressively reaching out for perspective. The objective of a "customer-centric" business, which is well intended if perhaps too limited in a multicentric world, is to make the customer's perspective a driving force within the business. Supply chain management is aimed at capturing the perspectives of vendors to maximize innovation and efficiency. The use of diversity training tools, such as "appreciative inquiry," is designed to capture the perspectives and insights of the entire workforce (see the sidebar discussion of the appreciative inquiry training approach).

The ultimate goal is *inclusivity*. I recently asked Mohanbir Sawhney, how to succeed as a learner. He ought to know. Mohan is the Tribune Professor of Technology and Director, Center for Research in Technology and Innovation at the Kellogg School. He has a Bachelor of Technology in Electrical Engineering, a Master's degree, and a Ph.D. in Marketing from the Wharton School of the University of Pennsylvania. He replied that you must encourage and pursue "the inclusion of different ideas from different people into your thinking."

Leaders build the corporate perspective by creating formal and informal mechanisms that encourage the sharing of individual perspectives. When Jeffrey Immelt became CEO of General Electric after Jack Welch's retirement, he injected more perspective into the company's strategic process. As each of the teams leading GE's business units create its plan, it is posted on an internal Web site and reviewed by approximately 50 executives from across the company's many businesses. "Sharing the multiple perspectives from diverse industries gives everyone new insights and ideas for further discussion and debate," write former CEO Larry Bossidy and consultant Ram Charan, who taught strategy during my student years at Kellogg. Perspective is again injected into the strategy process when the business unit teams meet at headquarters. "Outsiders," continue Bossidy and Charan, "with specific expertise in the political and regulatory arenas, global financial systems, technology, and the like are brought in to share their views and answer questions."

The concept of multitasking, that is, giving functional executives several jobs, provides another effective perspective-building strategy. When I was CFO at Hannaford Bros. Co., for example, I also had temporary responsibility for information systems and technology (IT). While I searched for a new chief information officer (CIO), I spent each Wednesday in a cubicle in the middle of the 125 people in the IT department and immersed myself in their issues, concerns, and perspectives. That experience proved to be invaluable in helping me understand the opportunities and challenges involved in connecting the strategy and day-to-day concerns of IT to the company's overarching goals and strategy. Today, we are seeing more and more executives with dual job responsibilities. CIOs are also running business units and human relation heads are also in charge of customer service. "It's a win-win for the company and the individual," says Carnegie-Mellon University professor Robert Kelley. "The more exposure to different kinds of business units, the more versatile, and hence more valuable, you become."

The most widely embraced strategy for building organizational perspective is summed up in the word "diversity." Although this word has evolved from the national mania on political correctness, the essence of diversity is inclusiveness and should not be dismissed. Inclusiveness is often the source of new perspectives and innovative thinking.

Diversity authorities argue that creating a workforce that includes a broad range of perspectives improves performance and profits. Indeed, there is much evidence that it does. In January 2004, Catalyst, a leading research and advisory organization founded in 1962, released the results of a study in which five years of financial results in 353 of nation's largest companies were correlated to the degree of gender diversity in their leadership teams. The results, as reported by *Business Week*, were surprising:

On average, companies with the highest percentage of women among their top officers had a return on equity 35.1% higher than those with the fewest high-level women. Total return to shareholders was 34% higher for companies with the most executive women, vs. those with the fewest.

Gender, of course, is not the only perspective to consider in enhancing returns to investors and evaluating companies' success. As companies' extend their global reach and aim for new markets, we have opportunities to better understand how ethnicity, age, religion, disability, and national origin can also contribute to organizational performance. Of course, U.S. companies must comply with legal requirements, but they may well find it worth the investment to exceed legal expectations in the development of an inclusive and welcoming business environment. In a Society for Human Resource Management/ *Fortune* survey of human resource professionals in Fortune 100 companies, 79 percent said their diversity initiatives improved the corporate culture, 77 percent said their initiatives improved recruitment, and 91 percent said their initiatives "helped their organizations stay competitive."

Leaders always play a fundamental role in encouraging inclusion. In fact, this is one area in which a single leader can have a tremendous impact. Claudine Malone is one of those leaders.

Claudine is a pioneering African-American businessperson. A graduate of Wellesley and Harvard Business School, she began her career at IBM and quickly gravitated toward teaching at various business schools and consulting. She has been and continues to be an active director on the boards of large companies. When Claudine joined the board of Limited Brands in the early 1980s, there were few women on the company's management team, even though women were the company's largest customer group.

As a director, Claudine is always working to build perspective into boards and senior leadership teams. One of her long-term goals has been to increase the number of females in the C-suite at each company in which she has served as director. She also encourages the companies she serves to appoint more female directors. Ten years after working with Claudine when she was a board member and I was the CFO of Hannaford Bros. Co., she initiated the suggestion and the contact that led to my directorship at Lafarge NA, the largest diversified construction materials supplier in the United States.

The challenge for FISO Factor leaders is to build on the example set by people like Claudine Malone. Identify those areas of your business that would most benefit from new perspectives. Create formal and informal programs that encourage inclusion and diversity. Put those new perspectives to work to grow your company.

APPRECIATIVE INQUIRY

One way to capture the power of perspective is to be appreciative. When you focus on the negative, people erect barriers. They hide, rather than share, their perspectives. Appreciative inquiry (AI), a technique conceptualized and created in 1987 by Dr. David Cooperrider, Suresh Srivastva, and their colleagues from Case Western Reserve University's Weatherhead School of Management, captures the energy that is released when people are allowed to express their perspectives in a positive framework.

Appreciative inquiry is both a process and a philosophy. AI approaches large-scale change by tapping into what Amanda Trosten-Bloom, a director at the Corporation for Positive Change, defines as "the collective wisdom, knowledge, strategies, attitudes, skills, and capabilities of the organization at its best." In an AI "summit," large groups, sometimes, entire organizations come together to focus on what is working well, dreaming up ideal futures, and acting to make those dreams a reality. It is a technique that more and more companies are using to create organizational visions, align stakeholders, and build new cultures.

Interestingly, this work on the "soft" side of business has profitable ramifications. "Later on, we would discover that production had increased, that quality measures had been enhanced, that turnover had gone down, that people had managed to cut costs in pretty dramatic ways," says Trosten-Bloom. "We've now begun to discover that you can go directly at financial improvements using an AI approach."

To learn more about the AI approach to discover and apply new knowledge and new ideas about key aspects of organizational life for my clients, I attended a seven-day intense workshop led by Jane Magruder Watkins and Bernard Mohr. Both recounted remarkable firsthand success stories throughout the world in various for-profit and nonprofit organizations. In addition, we reviewed extensive research, much of which is available at www.appreciativeinquiry.cwru.edu.

PERSPECTIVE YIELDS BALANCED JUDGMENT

The catalytic agent of perspective is an indispensable support in your effort to develop balanced judgment. FISO Factor leaders must possess a well-honed ability to judge. They are called upon to judge the regulatory environment, the marketplace, the needs of customers, the capabilities of employees, the demands of owners, and the competitive atmosphere.

The problem, of course, is that no one leader has the breadth and depth of perspective necessary to make all the judgments required by his or her position. (Those who believe that they do have this power have lost their sense of perspective.) It is other people's perspectives that enable you to create the 360-degree view you need to assess and evaluate situations and options. These perspectives provide the insight that aspiring leaders need to discern the many sides of every story, to evaluate and deliberate upon the most critical issues, and to identify, assess, and choose between the alternative responses that are possible in any given situation.

Among the many perspectives that aspiring leaders must seek out are the insights that enable them to fit-in. When Carly Fiorina started her tenure at H-P, she reached back to the roots of H-P to revitalize the company and create new growth. She fit in by connecting to the entrepreneurial "two guys in a garage" perspective that made H-P a great company in the first place and that its employees still revered.

The insights that leaders must discover in order to stand out may be found in the others' perspectives. When Lou Gertsner said "forget the vision thing" and refocused IBM on customers, he stood out by creating a new strategy based on customer perspectives. In the process, IBM was transformed from a stagnant products company into a service giant.

No one can make balanced judgments in a vacuum. The catalytic agent of perspective is the trait that enables FISO Factor leaders to develop the "big picture," reach sound decisions, and develop the support they need to act successfully. This is not to say that the catalyst of perspective can eliminate all errors—nothing can make us infallible. It can, however, significantly lessen the risk that is entailed in any change.

THE ABCS OF PERSPECTIVE

Here are some thought-starter questions for perspective.

Fitting In with Perspective

Attitude: Empathize with stakeholders. Are you identifying all the stakeholders before you reach a decision? Do you take the time to "walk in the shoes" of those people your decisions will affect?

Behavior: Keep your sense of perspective. Where does your perspective fit into the corporate universe? What other perspectives have as much or more influence on your company or business unit?

Characteristic: Acknowledge that your perspective is rarely complete. How often do you think that other people do not "get it"? Do you feel that you have an answer for every question?

Standing Out with Perspectives

Attitude: Always welcome a new perspective. How do you react when faced with bad news? How can you demonstrate that it is safe to share perspectives that might be unwelcome?

Behavior: Allow perspectives to emerge. What forums, either formal or informal, can you provide to solicit stakeholders' perspectives? How can you tangibly demonstrate your respect for and consideration of other people's perspectives?

Characteristic: Make space for those who have not traditionally had a place at the corporate table. What are the perspective gaps in your team? How can you hire or promote to close those gaps?

GLOBAL CITIZENSHIP: THE PASSPORT TO OPPORTUNITY

Americans expect to be allowed to travel to most parts of the earth and often exercise that desire as time and money permit. When passports were first issued by the U.S. Department of State starting in 1789, they simply facilitated international travel by certifying citizenship. In fact, except for wartime and other periods of national emergency, U.S. citizens were not legally required to obtain passports for foreign travel until 1952. Today, passports both facilitate and restrict our ability to travel freely. They ease our movement in and out of the United States and other nations. At the same time and with a few exceptions, we cannot move freely through the world without them. Whether you view your passport as an opportunity or a limitation is largely a matter of individual perception. The same is true for the rapidly expanding global economy.

Many businesspeople worry about the ramifications of the global economy. Some equate it with offshore sourcing, the theft of intellectual property, the counterfeiting of goods, and product dumping by foreign competitors. Some see economic globalization as a dangerous development that threatens the health of their companies and the stability of their workforces. Especially in times of war and terror alerts, some see a world full of enemies who want to harm their homeland, employees, and companies.

The fact that all of these troubling activities occur makes a xenophobic view of the world all the more difficult to dislodge. The dark side of globalization makes sensational headlines, so it can appear that the trend is solely a negative one. There is, however, another side to globalization. For instance, there are the benefits of what Nancy McLernon, deputy director of the Organization for International Investment, calls "insourcing." She reports that annual direct foreign investment in the United Sates totaled $82 billion in 2003. Further, the U.S. subsidiaries of foreign companies employ 6.4 million Americans. She also finds that while the outsourcing of American jobs grew at an annual rate of 3.8 percent; the annual growth rate of "insourced" jobs expanded at nearly double that pace, at 7.8 percent.

Globalization is also our passport to business opportunity. Two-thirds of the world's purchasing power and 95 percent of the world's consumers reside outside our national borders. The Department of Commerce calculated that the annual U.S. exports to China alone totaled $28.4 billion in 2003.

Global economy statistics like these compel business leaders in America's largest companies to consider providing goods and services to consumers and companies outside the U.S. boundaries. CEO Jeffrey Immelt devoted a half page to globalization in his "Letter to Stakeholders" in General Electric's 2003 Annual Report. After reporting a mere 1 percent rise in total revenues, a significant shortfall from the company's target of double-digit growth, he wrote:

We can take every growth idea and multiply its effectiveness through globalization. Globalization is a GE core competency. We have made and sold products outside the U.S. for 100 years, and one-third of our leadership team is global. Our global revenues were almost $61 billion in 2003, up 14%, and should grow 15% in 2004.

Globalization is controversial today. In fact, it is viewed in some quarters as un-American. I am proud to be an American CEO of an American company. But growing GE requires us to view the world as our market.

In fact, the *Wall Street Journal* reported in January 2005 that the top 25 U.S. companies made 43 percent of their revenue abroad.

The FISO Factor catalyst of global citizenship is the key to this world of opportunity. Global citizenship enables leaders to fit in no matter where in the world they choose to conduct business. Also, global citizens have the capacity to transform their organizations—a business imperative necessary to standing out.

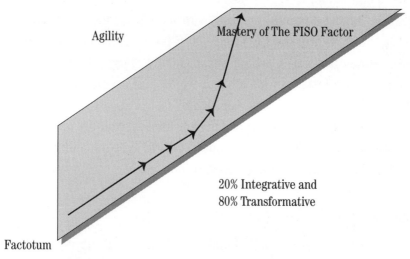

Figure 9-1   The Catalytic Spectrum for Global Citizenship

GETTING PREPARED FOR GLOBAL LEADERSHIP

When business is a global pursuit, leaders must be global citizens. You might argue that there are many leadership positions that do not require global savvy. You might argue that you work in a domestic company that does not buy goods and services from international suppliers, does not compete with international companies, and does not sell beyond the nation's borders. I would suggest, however, that you should be qualifying your statements with a hearty "at this time."

The world changes more rapidly every day. Communication and transportation technologies are shrinking the distances between nations and are sometimes transcending borders altogether. The global economy is already changing the way you shop, eat, and invest. Since every job, ranging from the low to high skilled, will be affected by globalization, it only makes sense that it will soon change the way you work. It is time to start thinking ahead.

Many aspiring leaders do not have the luxury of time. In 2003, I wrote a column for *CFO Europe* about a finance manager who came to me after having a painful meeting with his CEO. In spite of his good performance record, the CEO told him if he did not travel more often to the other nations in which the company operated, the manager could not be effective in his job and would lose credibility. This manager needed to become a global citizen fast. I suggested there were three leadership abilities he needed to develop: the ability to transcend nationality; the ability to learn from the world; and the ability to stimulate global coordination and cooperation.

Transcend Nationality

FISO Factor leaders are notable for their ability to transcend national boundaries. They do not abandon their national citizenship, but at the same time, they do not have a "center of the earth" orientation. That is, they attempt to understand their own national biases, assumptions, and cultural constraints, comparing them to other nations' biases, assumptions, and cultural constraints. They can seek out and enjoy contact with other cultures, learn everywhere in the world, and build international webs of cooperation. They strive to develop into global citizens.

David Thomas and Keer Inkson, management professors at Canada's Simon Fraser University and New Zealand's Massey University, respectively, define the ability to transcend nationality as "cultural intelligence," which they describe as consisting of three components:

- The *knowledge* to understand cross-cultural phenomena
- The *mindfulness* to observe and interpret particular situations
- The ability to adapt *behavior* to act appropriately and successfully in a range of situations

As Americans, we appear to have a natural *disadvantage* when it comes to cultural intelligence and, accordingly, to working effectively in the global arena. Management professor Karl Moore of Canada's McGill University found that nations with dominant positions in the world, such as the United States, Japan, and Germany, tend to produce fewer global managers than less powerful nations, such as Canada, Switzerland, and Belgium. Why? Moore explains: "Dominant countries become dominant because of their very success, and their achievements ought to be admired and applauded. There is a downside, however, to such size and success: It can cause managers of big firms in big countries to become complacent and begin to think that, for instance, the American shareholder is the only one that matters or that the Japanese keiretsu system [is] the only [way] to do business."

Conversely, Moore finds that global managers from midsized nations are naturally open to other cultures because of their position in the global hierarchy. They have learned to be global citizens because they have to adapt to other cultures to be successful. "It is a strength of Canada, Finland, the Netherlands, and others that citizens learn from the cradle to take into account other perspectives," says Moore. "We may not always agree, but we must listen and respect." From a firsthand perspective, Dutch and Finnish colleagues expect no one outside of their home countries to speak their native language. They learned early in life, the importance of foreign language if they wanted to expand their universe and horizons.

A global citizen attempts to eliminate national parochialism from his mindset and to embrace the world's diversity. In 2002, when I was spending one-third of my time in New York, one-third in Paris, and one-third traveling to BIC businesses around the world, an interviewer asked what I loved about working for a multinational company. I enthusiastically replied, "The exposure to different cultures. I deal with four continents, since we are in 160 countries, and I like the challenge of each culture." I consider the opportunity to meet and work with the people from around the world one of the great benefits of my career. Reflecting back, it is that attitude of curiosity that set the stage for developing the catalyst of global citizenship.

The development of global citizenship also requires that you demonstrate your willingness to embrace other cultures. As we saw in an earlier chapter, the fact that I made the effort to learn and speak French far outweighed the fact that my command of the language was imperfect. People respect an outsider's willingness to try to communicate with them on their terms. This is a fundamental lesson—one that stands behind decisions such as Siemens AG's mandate that all country managers must speak the local language.

Global citizenship further requires that you be sensitive to the cultural practices of others. Prior to my first visit to Japan, I learned that in that nation a person's business card represents the person. To fold it, doodle on it, or casually toss it into a desk drawer indicates a lack of respect. In Arab countries, to show another person the bottom of your shoe is an insult. So, be careful how you cross your legs.

These are simple points of etiquette that can smooth social relationships, but a keen awareness of cultural nuances can also mean the difference between career and corporate success and failure. As BIC's CFO, I quickly learned that France's financial community does not value the "underpromise, overdeliver" mode of results reporting to the same extent as U.S. investors. In France, stability, family reputation, and government financial backing can be more highly regarded than quarterly earnings results when deciding to invest in a company. Knowing this helped me adjust my messages to investors and analysts in the Euronext financial markets to reflect those priorities.

Cultural differences can also affect how you approach and succeed at organizational change. Thomas Sattelberger, formerly executive vice president of Lufthansa Airlines, found that when it comes to change, Americans are "naïve in a positive way," meaning, they respond to top-down driven efforts featuring the positive messages and the commitment of senior leaders. In Germany, particularly after the horrific events of the 20th century, people "are less inclined to follow a leader's proclamations regarding change," according to Sattelberger. There, change is best started at the edges of the organization with small, pilot programs and demonstrated successes. Global managers who ignore such realities decrease their odds of success.

STARTING ON THE GLOBAL JOURNEY

You don't have to get an international assignment to start developing the catalyst of global citizenship. Try some of these simple first steps:

- Join a nonprofit international affairs organization in your city such as The Chicago Council on Foreign Relations.

Visit the World Affairs Councils of America Web site for a listing of its local affiliates (www.worldaffairscouncils .org).

- Learn the foreign language of your choice. It is not absolutely essential for global success, but it will give you the boost you need to capture a future assignment. Knowing a language also reveals culture attitudes and nuances, enriching your appreciation of the people and their meanings.
- Tap into the resources of your alma mater. Universities and business schools offer courses and seminars in international business; professors and fellow alumni from foreign nations are valuable linkages.
- Tune into international news. Read the international coverage in magazines and newspapers; watch news programming from other countries, such as the BBC, and regularly read *The Economist* magazine.
- Stay in contact with international friends and colleagues. Their ideas and insights offer an enjoyable and informal means of keeping a global perspective.

Learn from the World

FISO Factor leaders exhibit their expertise as global citizens through their open approach and ability to learn across cultures. Like any effective learner, global citizens know that they do not know it all. They understand that different cultures can often be the source of valuable lessons. They are always seeking to recognize and capitalize upon the learning opportunities inherent in a global orientation. They are explorers—ambassadors of learning whose priorities include getting out into the world in order to discover new things.

Bruno Angelici, executive VP, Europe, Japan, Asia/Pacific and RoW (rest of world) at AstraZeneca PLC, is a fine example of a leader who learns from the world. Bruno was born in France and earned his MBA at the Kellogg Graduate School of Management, where we first met. He began his career in the pharmaceutical industry in the United States, moved back to France, and then, onto Japan, where he served as regional vice president for AstraZeneca. Now he is based in London at corporate headquarters. "The effort required to adapt yourself to a foreign environment, especially when it is in a country which is not speaking your own language, is a challenge which helps you to grow faster," says Bruno. "I would argue that in matters of personal growth you achieve more in a three-year international assignment than in six years of comfortable domestic home life."

Further, Bruno confirms that companies both large and small are becoming more global in nature. "It is more and more critical for managers to be able to work with and to manage people coming from different parts of the world who have different cultures and different ways of thinking," he warns. "Only international experience can prepare you adequately for this situation."

My own experience echoes Bruno's findings. In the early 1990s, while in my thirties, my job as chief administrative officer for Sara Lee's Pacific Rim Group included responsibility for diverse functions, including finance, strategy, management information systems, and human resources in Asia, Australia, and South America. Because the company was growing its operations in the region through an aggressive acquisitions program, I had the opportunity to work closely with many business leaders, often entrepreneurs and the owners of family-held companies, in many nations throughout the region. The experience was a never-ending source of business lessons that it is highly unlikely I would have learned in a position that kept me in the company's Chicago headquarters.

Many managers and executives attempt to avoid international assignments. Some are loath to leave the corporate power center. Some want to insulate themselves and their families from the often-difficult task of adjusting to new cultures. Yet, aspiring leaders who refuse international assignments insulate themselves from a valuable source of innovation and inspiration. Henry "Hank" McKinnell, CEO and chairman of Pfizer, Inc., the $45 billion pharmaceutical giant, found his overseas assignments a great source of learning. A native of Canada, McKinnell spent 14 years early in his career working overseas. "Overseas, you tend to get more functional experience at a younger age," says the CEO. McKinnell was country manager of Iran at age 28. He calls it a small operation, but notes that he gained manufacturing, sales, marketing, and clinical development experience. "I was running a mini Pfizer," he says.

McKinnell says that his exposure to other cultures offered important lessons that he now applies as a CEO. The Japanese emphasis on consensus taught him how to build coalitions and move groups. He applied the traditional hospitality toward strangers found in many Middle Eastern cultures to customer relations. "I've had hundreds of experiences I'll never forget," says, McKinnell. "They were invaluable in shaping me into the manager of a global company."

Stimulate Global Coordination and Cooperation

The final trait that enables aspiring leaders to capture the catalyst of global citizenship is their ability to stimulate coordination and cooperation across national borders. FISO Factor leaders mold far-flung international business units into the kind of lean, responsive, and integrated organizations you would expect to find if they were working together on the same project in the same time zone. They open superhighways between international units through which strategy, knowledge, and data can stream back and forth.

In the past, the relationship between international business units and corporate headquarters in the home country was often very simplistic. Products and sales targets were pushed out to the world; profits were pulled back in. Unless a problem cropped up, neither party had much to do with the other. This relationship is totally inadequate in an era of transnational corporations, which rely, as McKinsey and Company says, "on greater internal integration to capture global specialization and scale advantages and on local approaches to gain privileged access."

Leaders in these kinds of companies must ensure that their employees around the world move toward a shared mission. Successful employees must align with the common mission, values, strategies, and objectives of the organization. Pursuing common goals with common performance measures and operational standards ease communication and the delivery of results.This requires aspiring global leaders to be willing to travel and spend time communicating and developing trusting relationships in local business units around the world. Likewise, many non-U.S. employees benefit from the opportunity to visit the U.S. offices and cities. Once, after developing a solid working relationship with an employee at a South American subsidiary, he informed me of ongoing deception perpetrated by the company's local leaders. He had wanted to inform management prior to that, but did not know with whom to speak and more importantly, whom to trust.

Coordination also requires that local business units are well informed and focused on key measures and expected milestones to achieve corporate objectives. The South American employee who came to me with his problem was working in a company that had traditionally operated as a loose federation of entrepreneurial "fiefdoms." His local boss was the *patron* with whom he interacted at least five days a week, week in and week out. As the gradual globalization of the company's business grew, country managers and head office employees increased contact, communication, and coordination in order to move new products and services into myriad marketplaces as cost-effectively and efficiently as possible. Yet improper behavior impeded the bottom-line realization of this progress. Dismissing the *patron* and hiring new management who could uphold legal and company requirements depended upon building relationships with local employees. The veteran employees in the South American operations had never been asked to share systems and best practices and, indeed, had little incentive to cooperate. Since the corporate finance and operations managers had responsibility to build on best practices, they were the first to reach out to local management and vice-versa. As local managers and headquarters employees worked together in person, they developed trust and educated each other.

Finally, leaders must translate and transfer expertise no matter where in the world it originates. At BIC, one way I helped accomplished this was by holding annual meetings over a several-day period with approximately 100 key financial and information technology staff members stationed around the world. At one session, we worked together on developing ways to grow our business. The ideas varied considerably, but the most interesting ones tended to come from people who, in addition to being expert in BIC's procedures and processes, had applied their unique local perspectives to increase revenues incrementally. None of the ideas would have surfaced if we had not breathed the same air and broken bread together. The meeting itself also provided the impetus we needed to apply some of those ideas throughout the company.

When you get down to the nuts-and-bolts of this work of building an effective international organization, it is not all that different from building a great domestic organization. It is the long distances, the cultural diversity, and the widespread lack of international experience that make global management a more significant accomplishment. Learn to cope with those realities and you will quickly capture the power of global citizenship.

BUILDING THE GLOBAL ORGANIZATION

As the degree of economic globalization increases for the foreseeable future, companies will be forced to either follow the trend or be left behind. In 1999, McKinsey and Company calculated that "truly global markets now produce and consume 20 percent of the world output— about $6 trillion of the planet's $28 trillion gross domestic product." While domestic markets still absorb 80 percent of production output, creating a global business might appear optional. But, by 2027, according to McKinsey, these proportions will be reversed. Global markets will grow twelvefold and will comprise "more than 80 percent of world output." In that scenario, global business is an imperative.

Global Strategies

The fact that competitive advantage has an increasingly global quality has, of course, not been lost on companies with savvy and hard-working management and employees. These companies are busy building global strategies. Consider Wal-Mart Stores, Inc., the world's largest company with $256 billion in annual sales, and its initiatives in China. Wal-Mart's "Made in America" boast was a major marketing pitch back when Sam Walton was alive and still visiting consumers and employees in the stores. But now, more than 70 percent of the goods sold in the giant retail chain are manufactured in China. In fact, in 2004, the company announced that its purchases from China would hit $18 billion, roughly 10 percent of all Chinese exports to the United States, according to *Fast Company*.

At the same time, Wal-Mart is expanding into the Chinese marketplace as quickly as that government will allow. Wal-Mart entered the country in 1996 and in 2003, recorded $700 million in sales in China. By the end of 2004, it had 42 stores in 20 cities. Wal-Mart's excitement over

China is not hard to fathom. The Chinese retail market is estimated at $550 billion; in 20 years it could grow as high as $2.4 trillion. Carrefour and other retailers also established beachheads in China over the last decade—overcoming significant trade barriers.

Global Knowledge

Smart companies further realize that purchasing and selling are only two of the opportunities offered by globalization. Market, consumer, and product knowledge, suggests INSEAD professor Yves Doz, is perhaps the most valuable global asset. He says there are three core steps to capturing and profiting from knowledge on a global basis: a step of sensing, which is identifying and accessing existing knowledge . . . mobilizing, which is integrating scattered capabilities and emerging market opportunities in new products and services . . . [and] optimizing operations to maximize the return on these new offerings.

Microsoft Corporation searches the globe for the knowledge it needs to stay ahead of its competition. In 1998, it opened a large research center in China—one of the first by a multinational company. "China was really the No.1 target from the beginning. We felt there was a tremendously deep pool of talent there," says Richard Rashid, senior VP of Microsoft research. "There's an internationalization of research going on. That's a good thing. The more smart people, the more innovation, and the more benefit for companies like Microsoft." Today Research Asia employs 170 scientists.

In December 2004, Microsoft announced plans for a new research center in Bangalore, India. Some might interpret this as a simple case of off-shoring, but Rashid quickly disabused observers of that notion. "You don't start something like this because you believe it's going to be cheaper, not for basic research. You're doing it because you believe you can hire great people."

Moving operations abroad may reduce costs for some American companies, but this is not the only reason Americans are building international operations. American producers today confront a paucity of dependable, literate, and creative production employees, shortages of skilled workers, and a declining pool of management candidates with relevant international experience. Foreign operations help satisfy these needs.

Global Management

Finally, it is clear that when strategy and knowledge develop across wider and farther territories, management must also develop a broader horizon. FISO Factor leaders must develop a pool of leaders, who, like themselves, are global citizens. This necessity is already clear in hiring trends at the C-level.

In 2003, in the seventh annual "Route to the Top" survey conducted by *Chief Executive* and recruiting firm Spencer Stuart, "international experience" rose to the top of the list of CEO qualifications. Further, the survey found that 30 percent of the top 700 CEOs have international experience, a substantial increase over the 21 percent just a year before. "The value is clear," says Tom Neff, U.S. chairman of Spencer Stuart. "For CEOs, an experience overseas can provide a real competitive edge." International experience is also increasingly demanded of CFOs. In 2001, John Wilson, cohead of Korn Ferry's CFO practice, said that it is "probably number four or five on the [CEO wish] list at large-to-midcap companies."

How can you build a global management team and groom the next generation of leaders? International assignments are the most obvious way. Companies should be encouraging overseas travel and making it an established part of the career track. If your managers know they will not be able to advance to the top of the organization without international experience, there will be less resistance to overseas assignments.

Companies can also offer promising managers short-term international assignments, which are easier to accept. Offering such assignments to younger managers is also a good strategy. Employees who perceive themselves and their families to be more flexible will likely be more willing to travel overseas. Further, the intensive experience they gain will also benefit your company.

Cross-cultural training is a supplemental tool for building cultural intelligence. Companies need to build cultural awareness, knowledge, and sensitivity among all employees (see sidebar). Such training can pay dividends in the increasingly culturally diverse domestic workplace, as well as in international assignments. In 2000, the U.S. Census Bureau reported that fully one in four workers in the United States were foreign born. Thus, all managers can benefit from cross-cultural training.

READY FOR ECONOMIC GLOBALIZATION?

How well prepared is the next generation of business leaders to cope with a global economy? The National Geographic-Roper 2002 Global Geographic Literacy Survey of young adults (18–24 year olds) found that:

- Young Americans ranked second-to-last in geographical literacy among nine nations, including Sweden, Germany, Italy, France, Japan, Great Britain, Canada, and Mexico.
- Only 24 percent of young American adults could locate Saudi Arabia on a map of the Middle East/Asia.
- Only 37 percent of young American adults could locate Great Britain on a map of Europe.
- 29 percent of young American adults could not locate the Pacific Ocean on a world map.
- 30 percent of young American adults said that the United States has a population of 1 to 2 billion people

(roughly one-third the world's population and far higher than the 2002 population of approximately 290 million).

Clearly, these findings are shocking for a country that considers its populace to be educated. One of the immediate remedies and an important step to global citizenship is to study geography and know some history—develop a sense of context.

GLOBAL CITIZENSHIP YIELDS AGILITY

The catalytic agent of global citizenship is intimately related to linkages, learning, and perspectives—three of the previous FISO Factor catalysts. Global citizenship creates a valuable new source of linkages. It expands our learning opportunities, and it offers us insight from a world of perspectives. In a very real sense, the catalyst of global citizenship enables us to multiply the power of these three catalysts.

This relationship between the catalysts is why I say that global citizenship yields agility. It enables aspiring leaders to transcend the artificial borders that define nations. This transnational agility opens a world of new opportunity as well as a world of new resources to the FISO Factor leader.

The agility conferred by global citizenship helps aspiring leaders to fit in anywhere in the world. The ability to fit in enables them to understand the business implications inherent in other cultures and foreign markets. This is the basis for creating solid footholds in the new global economy.

The agility conferred by global citizenship is also a transformational element that FISO Factor leaders can apply to their careers and companies. We've seen that managers with cross-cultural skills and experience are in high demand and low supply. Aspiring leaders who have these features on their resumes will naturally stand out. Their companies will also benefit from their skills and experiences as the global economy continues to grow in the near and long term.

THE ABCS OF GLOBAL CITIZENSHIP

Here are some thought-starter questions for global citizenship.

Fitting In with Global Citizenship

Attitude: Broaden your horizons. What are the boundaries of your world view—your home town, your home state, North America, or, like Jeffrey Immelt, the entire world? How are your company and your job linked to the global economy?

Behavior: Create a global network. Who are the global citizens in your company? What informal and social linkages can you create in the nations in which your company operates?

Characteristic: Become geographically literate. What and where on the globe are the issues that might affect your business occurring? What are the characteristics and qualities of your company's individual international markets?

Standing Out with Global Citizenship

Attitude: Open international lines of communication within your organization. How can you better include the needs and opinions of overseas offices, customers, and suppliers in your decision-making process? How can you create functional connections with your peers in international business units?

Behavior: Become an international traveler. Are you prepared and is your company aware that you are willing to accept international assignments? What nations in which your company operates could you travel to on vacation? *Characteristic:* Be a cross-cultural learner. How can you build your understanding and sensitivity to other cultures? How can your associates from other cultures teach you to be a better leader?

EPILOGUE: CHOOSING YOUR PATH

Every book is a journey and if it is a good one, it creates positive change in the reader. The goal of this journey has been to discover and explore how to develop and apply the FISO Factor of leadership to achieve success in your business and in your life. I hope that as you end this journey, you embark on another, better equipped and enthusiastically impatient to enjoy a personal and organizational quest for more effective leadership and high performance.

In exploring the FISO Factor, we have answered three major questions:

- Who? The who of the FISO Factor is you, the aspiring leader; it is your company too.
- Why? The why of FISO Factor is the need to establish an intimate relationship between your company's success and your career. It

is the parallel imperatives of integration and transformation and of fitting in and standing out.

- What? The what of the FISO Factor is its composition. The elements of that composition are the six catalytic agents: financial acuity, integrity, linkages, learning, perspective, and global citizenship.

This epilogue addresses two final elements: the "when" and the "where" of the FISO Factor. These are ultimately "how" questions, which offer insight into how to know when to apply your talent for fitting-in and standing-out. The answers suggest how to choose where to apply your FISO Factor.

FIT IN OR STAND OUT?

Fitting-in and standing-out are mutually supportive actions, but successful leaders rarely exhibit both behaviors at the same time. Rather, they must pick and choose between the two. They build their effectiveness, and the effectiveness of their organizations, by sometimes fitting-in and sometimes standing-out. The when question addresses the considerations of FISO Factor timing: corporate culture and your position.

Corporate Culture

The first issue in timing is the overall corporate culture and environment in which you work. Every company has a personality. Some companies are staid and buttoned-down. Think of the old IBM. When Lou Gerstner had his first meeting with the top 50 IBM executives, he realized that every man in the room was wearing a white shirt, except him. (This observation was apparently widespread. Weeks later, at the second meeting of the same group, Gerstner was amused to find that he was only man in white shirt.) Other companies are freewheeling and fun-loving. Southwest Airlines purposely tries to hire people with a sense of humor. Company founder Herb Kelleher once said, "Anybody who likes to be called a 'professional' probably shouldn't be around Southwest Airlines."

The corporate personality offers one clue to FISO Factor timing and intensity. Conservative companies may well frown upon employees who stand out too much or too frequently. Conversely, informal companies may expect employees to stand out as much as they desire and whenever possible.

Corporate personality can give you initial insight into the appropriate FISO Factor timing, but it is not the only, or even the best, indicator you should consider. A better indicator can be found in your company's approach to the future and its values. In this context,"the future" is defined as the company's *ability* to embrace and sustain new ideas to create the 21st century's meaningful and valuable company; "values" is its *willingness* to embrace change, to "rock the boat" in its industry, its markets, and its approach to business. The accompanying matrix shows these two qualities.

	High		
Ability to Embrace and Sustain New Ideas		Li quid" (High Stand Out/ Low Fit In)	"Steam" (Stand Out)
		"Ice" (Fit In)	"Mud" (Low Stand Out/ High Fit In)
	Low		
		Traditional	*Visionary*

Values

175

In the bottom-left corner of the matrix, in the box labeled "Ice," the values of the organization are traditional and not very flexible. At the same time, the company's openness to new thinking is low. When the leadership has a strong sense of history, and procedures are done because they have worked in the past, this is a company that requires the individual to fit in if she wants to succeed. Standing-out in this environment is a highly suspect behavior and likely to be rejected.

In the upper-right corner, in the box labeled "Steam," the situation is just the opposite. Here, the leadership is visionary and willing to explore unknown territory, products, and methods. In addition, the organization quickly embraces new ideas, transmitting them to all corners of its business. This company expects its employees to stand out whenever possible. Fitting-in is the suspect behavior in this environment, where few things last long enough to become institutionalized.

The upper-left and the lower-right corners of the matrix call for a more mixed approach to the FISO Factor. In the upper-left corner, in the box labeled "Liquid," the company can embrace innovation and focus on the future needs of today's customers, but there is resistance to change. In this case, an aspiring leader can exhibit qualities that stand out, but must be sure to have established a secure position in the company first. This company will only allow you to undertake change if you are one of its most trusted leaders.

In the lower-right corner, in the box labeled "Mud," the organization is willing to accept change, but does not have the ability to create it or a clear vision of what the uncertain future may reveal. In this case, aspiring leaders must be focused more intently on fitting-in and should approach change very cautiously. This is a company that will allow you to undertake change, but one in which change probably will not occur with a successful outcome.

Position in Company

The second major consideration in FISO Factor timing is your position within the company. We need to fit in and we need to stand out to different degrees depending on our job responsibilities and our tenure within the company. So, while one behavior might earn you a promotion as a young manager, it can just as easily cause you to be out-placed later in your career.

It is, of course, impossible to cover every career situation, but there are some basic rules of thumb. You should probably be thinking about fitting-in, if you are just starting a new job. Even when you are being hired to shake up the business, you must fit in to some degree to gain support. If you are in the early years of your career, you should also be focused on fitting-in. In this situation, you need to establish your reliability and your credibility. Further, each industry has its own sense of the *duration* you must fit in before exhibiting stand-out traits. Think of the pace of change in a heavy equipment manufacturer compared to the nimble responsiveness required of a retailer who interacts with its customers daily.

Starting a new job, joining a new industry, or moving to a new country for a position should all be times when you focus on developing and mastering the foundational FISO Factor catalysts of financial acuity, integrity, and linkages. You want to demonstrate that you understand the language of business and that you are honest and trustworthy. You also should be creating the linkages that will enable you to stand out later.

In general, you should be focused on standing-out when you have become established in your position. When you have demonstrated that you can handle your everyday job responsibilities, it is a good time to stretch out a bit and attempt to drive performance gains. The middle and later years of your career are times to flourish and to stand out.

These are the times when you establish your ability and potential to lead in larger contexts.

These are also the times when you should be developing and mastering the transformational FISO Factor catalysts of learning, perspective, and global citizenship. You need to learn continually in order to renew your growth and avoid stagnation. As your leadership responsibility grows and you deal with more and more stakeholders, the importance of perspective and adjusting to deeper and increased levels of complexity also grows. And finally, as your company and your span of authority both expand across national borders, global citizenship becomes an imperative.

NAVIGATING THE JOURNEY

There is a scene in *Alice's Adventures in Wonderland* in which a very lost and bewildered Alice meets the Cheshire Cat. "Would you tell me, please, which way I ought to go from here?" she asks the grinning cat.

"That depends a great deal on where you want to get to," replies the cat.

"I don't much care where . . ." begins Alice.

"Then," interrupts the cat, "it doesn't matter which way you go."

It is one of the rare sensible statements that Alice hears in Wonderland. It is also soundly applicable to your leadership journey. You cannot evaluate the point of greatest leverage for your FISO Factor skills without knowing your long-term career goals. Thus, the most important variable in the "where" decision is the ability to clearly articulate what you want to achieve.

Actor Jim Carrey likes to tell this story: In the mid-1980s, when he was still struggling to establish his career, Carrey wrote himself a check "for acting services rendered" in the highly unlikely amount of $10 million—more than any actor had been paid for a role at that time. He put it in his wallet and carried it around for years. In 1995, he actually received $10 million for his role in the sequel to *Ace Ventura*.

Carrey's story has a dramatic flair, but it is true that goal articulation creates a sense of purpose and focus that can often appear magical. I decided I wanted a career in finance in my teens. When I entered the workforce in the late 1970s, I decided that I would become a CFO in a large company. At the time, I was not aware of a single female CFO in the Fortune 500. When I achieved that goal in 1994, I was still one of only ten female CFOs in the Fortune 500.

There are two lessons here: Set your goals and as important, shoot high. Do not settle for the easily achievable and do not set a goal that is a dollar amount—Carrey himself emphasizes that his check represented success as an actor, not money as an end in and of itself. As Daniel Hudson Burnham, an architect whose plans had a great influence on the development of Chicago, said, "Make no little plans; they have no magic to stir men's blood." Once you know where you want to go, the issue becomes how you evaluate your options. There are many paths to a successful career. John Dasburg, a fellow director for St. Paul Travelers Companies, earned a BA in engineering, joined the Navy, and then returned to school for an MBA and law degree before he entered the business world full-time at age 30. He became a partner at KPMG, joined Marriott in the hotel business, and then successfully led Northwest Airlines through a high-profile turnaround. He moved from the airlines to Burger King and most recently, led a group of private investors, which purchased ASTAR Air Cargo (formerly DHL Airways), where he serves as CEO and chairman. "My life demonstrates that there is no one path to success," said John, when he received the Horatio Alger Award in 2001.

The problem is that many aspiring leaders do not evaluate their options properly. Often, the career journey centers around whether and

179

how long to stay with a single employer. This discussion is largely a waste of time. In my experience, duration of employment is not a primary element in career success. I have moved between companies fairly regularly and so has John Dasburg. On the other hand, I also work with Susan Kronick, vice chair of Federated Department Stores, and Philippe Rollier, president and CEO of Lafarge NA, both of whom have been with the same large companies for decades. Both strategies can lead to success.

The other common red herring in the option evaluation process is money. Too many aspiring leaders chase a larger paycheck. Compensation may well be a higher priority early in a leader's career and it is always a consideration, but should not have too great an influence. On occasion, I have accepted lateral moves and even positions that did not pay what I thought they should have.

There are considerations more important than money. I like the way Arthur Martinez described his own reaction when Sears pursued him for its top spot. Martinez was in the final stages of accepting another job when the troubled retailer approached him. The compensation was roughly equal and he faced the prospect of a lawsuit if he backed out of the other job at such a late date. Nevertheless, he chose to join Sears. He explained his decision as follows:

> This would be the professional challenge of a lifetime. This would be the cap on a lifetime of preparation. It would be one thing to help a nice billion dollar mid-market department store come out of bankruptcy, but if the Sears thing could be done, forget about the money.

So, how should you navigate the intersections in your career journey? In 2003, during an interview, when I was asked how I evaluate offers to join boards, I replied with three questions that you can use to evaluate any career opportunity: Can I contribute to the success of the company? Will I learn something from this? Is the company ready to do what needs to be done? The answer to all three must be a resounding yes.

Can I Contribute to the Success of the Company?

A static opportunity is dead end opportunity. True leaders are not placeholders. Instead, they have a vision of a better future and work to move their organizations toward it.

You must think in terms of opportunity. I do not simply mean personal and professional opportunity. Too many aspiring leaders get mired in the "what's in it for me" mode. There is no hiding that attitude and it will stall your career. I am talking about the *opportunity to contribute* to an organization. This thought brings us in a full circle back to Chapter 1: Career success derives from corporate success.

The turning point in Lou Gertsner's decision to join IBM began with the realization that it was very likely that he could not contribute to the success of RJR Nabisco much longer—it was performing well, but it was too highly leveraged to deliver the returns expected by KKR (Kohlberg Kravis Roberts & Company), which had orchestrated the company's LBO just a few years before. Gerstner's second key realization was that his skills were a good match for IBM—that the company did not need a technology expert as much as an expert change agent. He realized that he could make a positive contribution at IBM.

Will I Learn Something from This?

Over the long term, perhaps the most important personal consideration in any career opportunity is its learning potential. When Susan Kronick described why she had spent her career at Federated, she said that every few years she had been offered new positions within the company that gave her fresh learning opportunities and new challenges. This opportunity for renewal and growth convinced Susan to turn down all offers from outside the company.

The content of your learning will, of course, change as your career progresses. In the early years, you should pursue opportunities that offer a sound fundamental education. Microsoft's Steve Ballmer and e-bay's Meg Whitman had the benefit of marketing training at Procter & Gamble early in their careers. In midcareer, you might look for opportunities that enable you to expand your horizons. I joined Sara Lee to gain international experience, and in my first week at work I happily found myself on a plane for the Paris office with the president of the company to review our European strategy for acquisitions and market development. Expanding your horizon, by definition, will provide new and different challenges. These are opportunities that enable you to stretch your capabilities—sometimes beyond limits you thought possible or probable.

THE LEADERSHIP LEARNING QUOTIENT

Good opportunities enable us to grow as leaders. In *The Leadership Pipeline*, Ram Charan, Stephen Drotter, and James Noel map six "passages" to increasing leadership responsibility:

Passage 1 is the transition from managing self to managing others.

Passage 2 is the transition from managing others to managing managers.

Passage 3 is the transition from managing managers to managing a function.

Passage 4 is the transition from functional manager to business manager.

Passage 5 is the transition from business manager to group manager.

Passage 6 is the transition from group manager to enterprise manager.

One test of an opportunity's viability is to identify your place among the six passages and determine if the new opportunity will enable you to implement and exercise your current expertise and developed abilities as well as allow you to learn the skills needed to advance to the next level of the leadership pipeline.

Is the Company Ready to Do What Needs to Be Done?

Companies must change in order to grow and remain healthy. But change is difficult and there are many companies that will not undertake it. Unfortunately, those that do not stagnate or become extinct.

When you evaluate an opportunity, you must determine if the company is capable of change and growth. You must decide for yourself whether the organizational conditions will allow you to contribute and make a difference. In the financial world we call this process "due diligence" and it applies just as well to career opportunities.

There are many possible issues in this due diligence. When I evaluate a consulting client, I begin by creating a portrait of the company. I consider its identity, customers and markets, core competencies, current positioning, competition, distribution channels, vulnerabilities, key selling point, and vision of future.

I try to gather this information from sources external to the company. This often involves research drawn from public sources as well as interviews with outside observers and past employees—anyone outside the company who has credible knowledge and direct observation. I also gather this information inside the company by interviewing and questioning the potential client. Then, I compare the external and internal information. If they jive with each other, I probably have an accurate portrait. If they don't, I know that caution is warranted.

What characteristics should you be looking for? Turn back to the six catalytic agents of the FISO Factor. You should be looking for the same qualities in companies that you are trying to develop in yourself: financial acuity, integrity, linkages, learning, perspective, and global citizenship. The important lesson: If a new opportunity will foster the development of your FISO Factor and at a pace similar to your own personality, then it will be a good combination for both you and your employer.

A FINAL WORD ON SUCCESS

The leadership journey is never a smooth one; it requires perseverance and tenacity. Further, the leadership path that you follow will surely be a unique one. I am convinced, however, that no matter which path you choose, the FISO Factor will be a driving force in your long-term success. The FISO Factor creates and supports both corporate success—enabling the integration and transformation that drives organizational growth and profitability—and career success—enabling you to fit in and stand out as an effective leader.

There is a wonderful quote, often attributed to Dale Carnegie: "Success is getting what you want; happiness is wanting what you get." It is my hope that this book helps you find both, in business and in life.

NOTES

Chapter 1

Page 2: *Of course, by the very structure of the corporate pyramid* . . . Richard S. Wellins and Patterson S. Weaver, Jr., "From C-Level to See-Level Leadership," *T+D Magazine*, September 2003, page 61.

Page 2: *Consider the retained executive search industry* . . . Industry figures for retained executive search firms are available from the Association of Executive Search Consultants, www.aesc.org.

Page 2: *In 1997, about half of the respondents* . . . Ann Barrett and John Beeson, *Developing Business Leaders for 2010* (The Conference Board, 2002), page 5.

Pages 2–3: *Developmental Dimensions International (DDI)* . . . Leadership Forecast :2003–2004:Executive Summary, www.ddiworld.com, page 2.

Page 4: *If I were to give advice* . . . John D. Rockefeller, *Random Reminiscences of Men and Events* (Sleepy Hollow Press, 1984), page 93.

Page 5: *Employers try to help.* . . . Holly Dolezalek, "The 23rd Annual Industry Report," *Training*, October 2004, page 28.

Page 6: *This lack of preparation . . . ten attributes that leaders will have to possess* . . . Ann Barrett and John Beeson, *Developing Business Leaders for 2010* (The Conference Board, 2002), page 6.

Page 8: *Parmalat, the global dairy food giant* . . . Gail Edmondson, "How Parmalat Went Sour," *BusinessWeek*, January 12, 2004, pages 46–48.

Page 9: *There is a dark side to this picture* . . . For an excellent analysis of Apple's struggle to produce profits from innovation, see Carleen Wood, "If He's So Smart . . .Steve Jobs, Apple, and the Limits of Innovation," *Fast Company*, January 2004, page 68.

Page 10: *This lesson made management thinkers* . . . See Chapter 7 of W. Edwards Deming's *The New Economics for Industry, Government and Education* (MIT Center for Advanced Engineering Studies, 1993).

Page 10: *Peter Senge, who introduced the concept of . . . "It is the discipline. . . ."* . . . Peter M. Senge, *The Fifth Discipline* (Doubleday Currency, 1990), page 12.

Page 10–11: *Senge found that systems thinking* . . . Senge, page 68.

Page 15: *After several more leadership missteps, AT&T* . . . For a trenchant analysis and insider's view of AT&T's struggle, see Dick Martin's *Tough Calls* (Amacom, 2004).

Page 15: *After several more leadership missteps, AT&T . . . "will likely be unable . . . available."* . . . "AT&T to Stop Competing in the Residential Local and Long-Distance Market in Seven States," corporate press release, June 23, 2004 (www.att.com/news/item/0,1847,13121,00.html).

Page 15: *A singular focus on transformation* . . . Tom Kelley, *The Art of Innovation* (Doubleday Currency, 2001), page 278.

Page 15–16: *The rush for Internet gold* . . . For a profane tour of the Internet carnage, see Philip Kaplan's *F'd Companies: Spectacular Dot-com Flameouts* (Simon & Schuster, 2002).

Chapter 2

Page 22: *I define authority as conferred power* . . . Ronald A. Heifetz, *Leadership Without Easy Answers* (Harvard University Press, 1994), page 57.

Page 24: *The process of fitting-in helps* . . . Jim Kouzes and Barry Posner, *Credibility* (Jossey-Bass, 1994).

Page 24–25: *It can be stated in one sentence* . . . As quoted in Theodore Kinni, "The Credible Leader," *Industry Week*, June 20, 1994, pages 25–26.

Page 26: *We found those who were promoted* . . . George W. Dudley, "The Importance of Managing Visibility," *Behavioral Sciences Research Press*, 2002, page 3.

Page 26: *Dudley's research team has replicated* . . .Dudley, page 3.

Page 26–27: *If you can muster that courage* . . . *"Great question . . . out of 'the pile.'"* . . . John C. Maxwell, *Thinking for a Change* (Warner Business Books, 2003), page 16.

Page 28: *Leaders such as Jack Welch* . . . Michael Maccoby, "Narcissistic Leaders: The Incredible Pros, the Inevitable Cons," *Harvard Business Review*, Jan–Feb 2000 (www.maccoby.com/articles/narleaders.html).

Chapter 3

Page 33–34: *Mystics in Europe and the Middle East practiced alchemy* . . . See Allen G. Debus, "Alchemy," *The Dictionary of the History of Ideas* (http://etext.lib.virginia.edu). Also, "Alchemy," Wikipedia (http://en.wikipedia.org/wiki/alchemy).

Page 35: *Scientists use catalysts* . . . See *The American Dictionary of the English Language*, Third Edition (Houghton Mifflin, 1996).

Page 37: *Marriott had become a major* . . . *"We took a major hit . . . business media,"* . . . J. Willard Marriott, Jr., *The Spirit to Serve* (Harper Business, 1997), pages 100–101.

Page 37–38: *It was Bollenbach who introduced* . . . *"virtually debt-free, . . . Marriott enterprise."* . . . Marriott, *The Spirit to Serve*, page 103.

Page 38: *It was Bollenbach who introduced* . . . *"In the aggressive atmosphere . . . management and service."* . . . Marriott, *The Spirit to Serve*, page 104.

Page 38: *Bollenbach became the CEO* . . . Ronald Henkoff, "Hilton vs. ITT: It Ought to Be No Contest," *Fortune*, March 3, 1997.

Page38: *Former Chairman and CEO of Honeywell* . . . Larry Bossidy and Ram Charan, *Confronting Reality* (Crown Business, 2004), page 216.

Page 38: *People often use the phrase* . . . Bossidy and Charan, page 4.

Page 40–41: *This seemed a responsible and ethical* . . . Quoted in Matthew Herper, "Merck Withdraws Vioxx," *Forbes.com*, September 30, 2004.

Page 41: *By mid-November, Merck stock* . . . Barry Meier, "Earlier Merck Study Indicated Risks of Vioxx," *NYTimes.com*, November 18, 2004; Robert Steyer, "The Murky History of Merck's Vioxx," *TheStreet.com*, November 18, 2004; "Merck: Vioxx Pulled When Risk Was Seen," *CNNMoney.com*, November 16, 2004.

Page 42: *What really distinguishes high performers* . . . Rob Cross, Thomas H. Davenport, and Susan Cantrell, "The Social Side of Performance," *MIT Sloan Management Review*, Fall 2003, page 20.

Page 42: *All of these creative linkages* . . . Disney Institute, Be Our Guest (Disney Editions), pages 16–17. See also Michael Eisner, *Work in Progress* (Hyperion, 1998) and Ron Grover, *The Disney Touch* (McGraw-Hill, 1997).

Page 43: *In March 2004, Roy Disney led* . . . See Laura Holson, "At Disney, Mending Fences or Moving On?" *NYTimes.com*, September 13, 2004; also Roy E. Disney's website *SaveDisney.com*.

Page 44: *One of the components of disciplined thought* . . . See Chapter 4 in Jim Collins, *Good to Great* (Harper Business, 2001).

Page 44–45: *What holds true for companies* . . . "The Narrow Path to Leadership," *Optimize*, August 2004.<Name of author to come>

Page 45: *This energetic, almost frenetic, focus* . . . See Chapter 16 in Noel M. Tichy and Stratford Sherman, *Control Your Destiny or Someone Else Will* (Harper Business, 1993).

Page 46: *Productivity is the belief that* . . . Quoted in Charles R. Day, Jr. and Polly LaBarre, "GE: Just Your Average Everyday $60 Billion Family Grocery Store," *Industry Week*, May 2, 1994, page 14.

Page 46: *This new perspective gave J&J pause* . . . Quoted in Lawrence G. Foster, *Robert Wood Johnson* (Lillian Press, 1999), page 621.

Page 47: *How can they overcome this dangerous habit?* . . . Michael Maccoby, "Narcissistic Leaders," *Harvard Business Review*, Jan/Feb 2000.

Page 48: *It is about winning a global tournament* . . . Yves Doz, José Santos, and Peter Williamson, *From Global to Metanational* (Harvard Business School Press, 2001), page 242.

Page 49: *Today, BIC is the world's leading maker* . . . Author interviews; see also the corporate history of BIC and a biographical sketch of Marcel Bich at www.bicworld.com.

Chapter 4

Pages 54–55: *What Pamela does know is business finance.* . . . Author interviews; Pamela Lieberman's presentation, Kellogg Leadership Forum, Evanston, IL, October 14, 2004; Andrew Carlo, "TruServ Weighs Options to Improve Profitability," *National Home Center News*, August 6, 2001; Andrew Carlo, "New Leaders to Take Helm at Two Co-ops," *National Home Center News*, December 17, 2001; "TruServ Completes Refinancing Agreement," *Rental Pulse*, September 8, 2003; Anna Marie Kukec, "TruServ Hopes New CEO on Board by '05," *Daily Herald*, November 5, 2004.

Page 57: *Allen himself was beginning to believe* . . . Dick Martin, *Tough Calls* (Amacom, 2004), page 000.

Page 59: *Read!* . . . For business finance, try Robert A. Cooke, *The McGraw-Hill 36-Hour Course in Finance for Nonfinancial Managers* (McGraw-Hill, 2004) and *Harvard Business Essentials: Finance for Managers* (Harvard Business School Press, 2002); for economics, try Charles Wheelan, *Naked Economics* (W.W. Norton, 2003).

Page 61: *For decades, many business leaders* . . . Quoted in Tom Brown, "A New Consciousness," *Leadership Now* (BNet.com), November 23, 2004.

Page 65: *You can also see Steve's predilection* . . . Quoted in Brent Schlender, "Ballmer Unbound," *Fortune*, January 26, 2004, page 123.

Page 67: *Kahl's emphasis on financial acuity paid off.* . . . Author interview; Michael A. Verespej, "He Did It His Way," *IndustryWeek*, November 20, 2000; Joshua Hyatt, "Steal This Strategy," *Inc*, February 1991.

Page 68: *Manco's larger brethren are also* . . . *"I want all employees to think like they are owners of the business,"* . . . Quoted in Matt Damsker, "Can You Hear Me Now?" *HR Innovator*, Jan/Feb 2004, page 21.

Pages 68–69: *Like Larry Bossidy, Honeywell's former chief,* . . . *"My first intuition was. . . . I decided to get out."* . . . Quoted in A.J. Vogl, "The Way It Is," *Across the Board*, May/June 2002, page 33.

Chapter 5

Page 72: *The North Star also has spiritual and mythical significance.* . . . See "North Star" in Wikipedia (http://en.wikipedia.org/wiki/north-star);

T.E. Shaw, translator, *The Odyssey of Homer* (Limited Editions Club, 1981), page 70; "Columbus and Celestial Navigation" (www1.minn.net/ ~keithp/cn.htm); "Follow the Drinking Gourd" (pathways.thinkport.org/ secrets/gourd1.cfm); Von Del Chamberlain, "The Chief Star," (www.clark-foundation.org/astro-utah/vondel/northstar.html); Julie Marshall, "New Show traces Pawnee star lore," *The Daily Camera*, April 25, 2002.

Page 72: *Kreuger was a business leader who . . .* Theodore Kinni and Al Ries, *Future Focus* (Capstone, 2000), pages 91–92.

Page 73: *76 percent of employees said . . . 2000 Organizational Integrity Survey: A Summary*, KMPG Integrity Management Services (www.us.kpmg.com/RutUS_prod/Documents/12/imsrvy_.pdf).

Pages 73–74: *Unsurprisingly, the crisis in trust . . .* "The Commission on Public Trust and Private Enterprise," The Conference Board Report, 2003, page 16, (http://www.conference-board.org/publications/reports.cfm).

Page 74: *British Lord Justice John Fletcher Moulton articulated . . .* John Fletcher Moulton, "Law and Manners," *Atlantic Monthly*, July 1924.

Page 75: *To be an effective catalyst . . . "steadfast adherence to strict moral or ethical code" . . .* See *The American Heritage Dictionary of the English Language: Third Edition* (Houghton Mifflin, 1996) for the three definitions of integrity.

Page 75: *To be an effective catalyst . . . This means that first . . .* See James O'Toole's *The Executive Compass* (Oxford University Press, 1993) for a brilliant exposition on the proper values of business leaders.

Page 75: *Ethics is a key quality in long-term leadership success . . .* Robert J. Thomas and Warren Bennis, "The Ambidextrous CEO," Accenture Research Note, December 30, 2002 (www.accenture.com/xd/xd.asp?it= enweb&xd=_ins\researchnote_180.xml); see also Warren Bennis and Robert J. Thomas, *Geeks & Geezers* (Harvard Business School Press, 2002).

Pages 75–76: *Harvard Business School professor Donald Sull . . .* Donald N. Sull, *Revival of the Fittest* (Harvard Business School Press, 2003), pages 116–117.

Page 76: *The second facet of . . . American Heritage Dictionary of the English Language*, Third Edition.

Page 76: *We can sense soundness in our leaders. . . .* Buffett's annual messages are available online at www.berkshirehathaway.com; see also

Andrew Kirkpatrick, *Of Permanent Value: The Story of Warren Buffett* (AKPE, 2005).

Page 78: *The third facet of integrity* . . . American Heritage Dictionary of the English Language: Third Edition.

Page 79: *Completeness is also recognizing* . . . Author interview; also "Raise the Bar," *NACS Magazine*, August 2002, pages 29–33.

Page 81: *Eventually, Deloitte and Touche investigated* . . . Alix Nyberg, "Whistle-Blower Woes," *CFO*, October 2003, page 64; "Vital Signs Denies Accounting Irregularities," *Accountancy*, December 5, 2003; Stephen Taub, "Vital Signs Settles with Former CFO," *CFO.com*, July 13, 2004.

Page 81: *St. Ignatius's Test* . . . See *The Spiritual Exercises of St. Ignatius* (www.ccel.org/ignatius/exercises.all.html).

Page 82: *In addition to constant vigilance over their integrity* . . . Jeffrey Sonnenfeld, "The CEO Blues," *Wall Street Journal*, December 9, 2003.

Page 83: *As the largest, and possibly most visible* . . . CEO message, Wal-Mart Stores, Inc. Annual report, 2004 (www.walmartstores.com).

Page 84: *Creating an intense organizational focus on integrity* . . . *"help them understand the line between aggressive business practice and improper activity."* . . . Quoted in Brian Hindo, "Face Time: Nancy Higgins" *BusinessWeek*, November 3, 2003.

Page 84: *Creating an intense organizational focus on integrity* . . . *Abbott Laboratories . . . business practices.* . . . Abbott Laboratories Pleads Guilty to Felony, Pays $600 Million," *Ethics Newsline*, July 28, 2003; Jason Compton "Abbott Laboratories' Shocking Ethics Gambit," *CRM*, October 2004, page 51.

Page 84: *In his study of reputational capital* . . . Kevin Jackson, *Building Reputational Capital* (Oxford University Press, 2004), pages 77–79.

Page 85: *Employee education is not the only support* . . . Neeli Bendapudi, "The Wow in Wawa," *NACS Magazine Supplement*, November 2004, page 6.

Page 86: *Silence is the enemy of integrity.* . . . Claudia H. Deutsch, "Corporate Silence Has a Vocal Opponent," *New York Times*, August 3, 2003.

Chapter 6

Page 89: *No one knows who discovered the lever* . . . Archimedes' quote was captured for posterity in the writings of Pappus of Alexandria; see *Bartlett's Familiar Quotations*: Sixteenth Edition (Little Brown, 1992).

Page 90: *The connections between people* . . . Wayne Baker, *Achieving Success Through Social Capital* (Jossey-Bass, 2000), page 1.

Page 90: *Baker ascribes significant advantages* . . . Baker, pages 9–19.

Page 91: *My professional link with* . . . Suzanne Fairlie, "Crisis of Competence" *HR Innovator*, Nov/Dec 2004, page 21.

Page 93: *Creativity is often seen as a mysterious process* . . . For a biographical sketch of Archimedes, see www.bbc.co.uk/history/historic_figures/archimedes.

Page 94: *Linkages are an important source* . . . Burt is quoted in Michael Erard, "Where To Get a Good Idea: Steal It Outside Your Group" *New York Times*, May 22, 2004.

Page 94: *People with connections across structural holes* . . . Ronald S. Burt, "Structural Holes and Good Ideas" *American Journal of Sociology*, September 2004, pages 349–399.

Page 95: *Often, the linkages that can best bolster* . . . Art Kleiner, *Who Really Matters* (Doubleday, 2003).

Pages 95–96: *The recognition of the importance of internal linkages* . . . Quoted in Joann S. Lublin, "How to Win Support from Colleagues at Your New Job" *The Wall Street Journal*, November 25, 2003.

Page 97: *To be sure breadth is important.* . . . Theodore B. Kinni and Al Ries, *Future Focus* (Capstone, 2000), page 9.

Page 99: *Create a robust network of linkages.* . . . Bill George, "The Journey to Authenticity" *Leader to Leader*, Winter 2004.

Page 99: *Create links in your community.* . . . Blythe J. McGarvie, "Networking for Success," unpublished manuscript, based on an interview with Meg Weston.

Page 99: *Don't Underestimate the Strength of Weak Ties.* . . . Mark S. Granovetter, "This Week's Citation Classic" *Current Contents*, December 8, 1986; Mark S. Granovetter, "The Strength of Weak Ties, *American Journal of Sociology*, May 1973, pages 1360–1380; also Albert-László Barabási, *Linked* (Plume, 2003), pages 41–44.

Pages 100–101: *If you are reluctant to give* . . . Quote in Betsy Wiesendanger, "Will You Do Me a Favor?" *Selling Power*, November/December 2003, page 34.

Page 101: *Networking Tactics* . . . The Pepsi Bottling Group's Diverse Leaders Conference was held at the Hyatt Regency, Greenwich, CT, July 13–14, 2004.

Pages 103–104: *Companies that act as if they are closed networks* ... James E. Rauch and Alessandra Casella, editors, *Networks and Markets* (Russell Sage Foundation, 2001), page 63.

Page 104: *The Secret Behind Viral Marketing* ... *Although viral marketing is a new strategy* ... Jean-Luc Cyrot, Christian Urdall, and Ignacio Garcia Alves, "Networks Work" *Prism*, 2/2003, pages 74–75.

Pages 104–105: *The Secret Behind Viral Marketing* ... *In 1982, Tom Peters and Bob Waterman* ... Stuart Crainer, *Corporate Man to Corporate Skunk* (Capstone, 2001); Ann Harrington, "The Big Ideas" *Fortune*, November 22, 1999.

Page 105: *One of the major issues that has emerged* ... Wayne Baker, "Building Collaborative Relationships" *Leader to Leader*, Spring 2003, page 15.

Page 105: *In another example of how existing* ... Thomas Claburn, "The Network That Really Matters," *Information Week*, March 8, 2004, pages 53–54.

Page 106: *Business problems require business solutions* ... This section is based on a working paper titled "Valuing and Managing the Return on Relationships" by Danny Ertel, Blythe McGarvie, and Jeff Weiss (Vantage Partners, 2001).

Page 107: *Iansiti and Levien point to* ... Marco Iansiti and Roy Levien, *The Keystone Advantage* (Harvard Business School Press, 2004), page 1.

Chapter 7

Page 109: In 1513, *Juan Ponce, better remembered as Ponce de Leon* ... Paul E. Hoffman, "Ponce de Leon, Juan" *American National Biography Online*, 2000 (www.anb.org/articles/20/20-00274.html); Ventura Fuentes, "Ponce de Leon" *The Catholic Encyclopedia*, 1913 (www.newadvent.org/cathen/12228a.htm).

Page 110: *So I began to force myself to study* ... Peter F. Drucker, "My Life as a Knowledge Worker," *Inc.*, February 1997 (www.inc.com/magazine/19970201/1169.html).

Page 113: *Some individuals may know this* ... Morgan W.McCall, Jr., Michael M. Lombardo, Ann M. Morrison, *The Lessons of Experience* (Lexington Books, 1988), pages 168–169.

Page 113: *I make it a policy never to miss an opportunity* ... Peter Drucker's speech at The Concours Group Conference, Pebble Beach, CA, August 6–8, 2001.

Page 114: *The study of demographics represents only one* ... Howard Schultz's presentation at The BusinessWeek 50 Forum, New York, NY, October 7, 2004.

Page 114: *A simple piece of data can also alert us* ... *Jeff Bezos started* ... Thaddeus Wawro, *Radicals & Visionaries* (Entrepreneur Press, 2000), page 40.

Page 114: *A simple piece of data can also alert us* ... *How did Howard Schultz discover Starbucks?* ... Wawro, pages 370–371.

Page 114: *A simple piece of data can also alert us* ... *How did Ray Kroc discover McDonalds?* ... Wawro, pages 250–251.

Page 115: *Aspiring leaders should always be asking* ... Jeff Thull, *Mastering the Complex Sale* (Wiley, 2003), pages 52–53.

Page 115: *There are times when a "why" question* ... Cathy A. Higgins and David J. Kreischer, "Leading Questions," *The StraightTalk Coach*, Vol. 1, Issue 7 (http://www.lifgroup.com/7a.pdf).

Page 116: *It is amazing how clearly things appear* ... Wawro, page 388.

Page 118: *Four Learning Skills* ... David A. Garvin, *Learning In Action* (Harvard Business School Press, 2000), pages 215–220.

Pages 119–120: *Starbucks' Howard Schultz likes to tell the story* ... Howard Schultz's presentation at The BusinessWeek 50 Forum, New York, NY, October 7, 2004; also Abrahm Lustgarten, "A Hot, Steaming Cup of Customer Awareness" *Fortune*, November 15, 2004.

Page 120: *So, take some time to think about the information* ... Quotes are drawn from Roderick M. Kramer, "The Harder They Fall," *Harvard Business Review*, October 2003, page 9.

Page 122: *There are many noteworthy change process texts and models.* ... I recommend John Kotter, *Leading Change* (Harvard Business School Press, 1996); William Bridges, *Managing Transitions* (Perseus, 1991); Harvard Business Essentials, *Managing Change and Transition* (Harvard Business School Press, 2003).

Page 124: *Successful leaders evaluate and learn* ... Drucker, "My Life as a Knowledge Worker."

Pages 125–126: *Sawhaney on Learning* ... Author interview at the Kellogg Innovation Network Annual Summit in Chicago, IL, October 20-21, 2004.

Page 126: *The concept of the learning organization* . . . Peter M. Senge, *The Fifth Discipline* (Doubleday Currency, 1991), page 4.

Page 126: *You do not have to take de Geus's word* . . . Laurie Bassi and Daniel McMurrer, "Are Employee Skills a Cost or an Asset?" *Business Ethics*, Fall 2004, pages 19–22.

Page 127: *Every day, every week I challenge* . . . Quoted in Martha Finney, "The Arte of Vegas HR" *HR Innovator*, March 2004, page 18.

Page 127: *Another strategy to encourage organizational learning* . . . Quoted in Carol Hymowitz, "The Best Innovations Are Those That Come From Smart Questions" *Wall Street Journal*, April 13, 2004.

Page 128: *Finally, it also makes good sense* . . . Quoted in John Foley, "Microsoft Tries to Buddy Up To ISVs" *Information Week*, July 12, 2004, page 24.

Pages 128–129: *The application of learning to the process of fitting-in* . . . Dick Martin, *Tough Calls* (Amacom, 2004), page 113.

Page 129: *Learning itself is the process by which* . . . Larry Bossidy and Ram Charan, *Confronting Reality* (Crown Business, 2004), pages 203–205.

Chapter 8

Page 131: *In the summer of 1664, Isaac Newton* . . . Michael White, *Isaac Newton: The Last Sorcerer* (Addison-Wesley, 1997), pages 58–60.

Pages 131–132: *Just as light is composed of a spectrum of colors* . . . The case is based on author interviews and e-mail with John Cahill, CEO of The Pepsi Bottling Group.

Page 134: *Around 600 B.C., Greek stone carvers* . . . See *Bartlett's Familiar Quotations*: Sixteenth Edition (Little Brown, 1992).

Pages 134–135: *The loss of perspective causes leaders* . . . Megan Barnett, "Leona Helmsley" *USNews.com*, August 16, 2004; also Rachael Bell, "Leona Helmsley, the Notorious Queen of Mean" *Court TV's Crime Library* (www.crimelibrary.com/criminal_mind/leona_helmsley).

Page 135: *The problem with losing your perspective* . . . "Stewart convicted on all charges" *CNNMoney.com*, March 5, 2004; also Brooke A. Masters, "Stewart Asks Judge to Let Her Begin 5-Month Sentence" *Washington Post*, September 16, 2004.

Pages 135–136: *William H. Macy, the actor and screenwriter* . . . . James Lipton's interview with William H. Macy, *Inside the Actor's Studio*, October 24, 2004.

Page 138: *Maintaining an empathetic connection* . . . Quoted in Justin Martin, "Rise of the New Breed" *CEO Magazine*, August/September 2003, page 27.

Page 139: *"I look to others quite frequently.* . . . Author interviews and e-mail with Joe Forehand, Chairman, Accenture, Ltd.

Page 139: *The effort a leader expends in his search* . . . Quoted in William Holstein, "Buffing the Image of the Chief Executive" *New York Times*, August 29, 2004.

Page 140: *I have never been content with the standard performance review .* . . Our interview appeared in Bill Birchard's "CFOs on Review" *CFO*, September 1997, pages 49–50.

Page 141: *HP people became concerned that Fiorina* . . . Thomas J. Neff and James M. Citrin, *You're In Charge—Now What?* (Crown Business, 2004), page 225.

Pages 141–142: *I usually have gathered others in an informal setting* . . . Robert Chuck's response to author e-mail, December 7, 2004.

Page 143–144: *I had to find opportunities to meet with people* . . . Charles O. Rossotti, *Many Unhappy Returns* (Harvard Business School Press, 2005), pages 88–89.

Page 144: *Recognizing the Six Perspectives on Change* . . . Jim Selman, "Leadership and Innovation" *The Innovation Journal*, December 12, 2002 (www.innovation.cc/discussion-papers/selman.pdf).

Page 146: *Leaders build the corporate perspective by creating* . . . Larry Bossidy and Ram Charan, *Confronting Reality* (Crown Business, 2004), pages 181–182.

Pages 146–147: *The concept of multitasking* . . . *"It's a win-win for the . . . you become."* . . . Quoted in Steven Marlin, "Double Duty" *Information Week*, November 8, 2004, page 46.

Page 147: *On average, companies with the highest* . . . Kimberly Weisul, "The Bottom Line on Women at the Top" *BusinessWeek Online*, January 20, 2004.

Page 148: *Gender, of course, is not the only perspective* . . . See the 2002 SHRM Fortune Survey on the Changing Face of Diversity (www.shrm.org).

Pages 149–150: *Appreciative Inquiry* . . . Author interviews; see also Amanda Trosten-Bloom and Diana Whitney, *The Power of Appreciative Inquiry* (Berrett-Koehler, 2003).

Chapter 9

Page 153: *Americans expect to be allowed to travel* . . . Russell D. Stetler, Jr., "Freedom to Travel" *Left and Right*, Spring 1966, pages 58–72; see also National Archives and Records Administration, "Passport Applications" (www.archives.gov/research_room/genealogy/research_topics.html).

Page 154: *The fact that all of these troubling activities occur* . . . Nancy McLernon, "Inside Outsourcing," *Robb Report*, July 2004, page 36.

Page 154: *Globalization is also our passport* . . . Sharon Lynn Kagan and Vivien Stewart, "International Education in the Schools," *Phi Delta Kappan*, November 2004 (www.pdkintl.org/kappan/k_v86/k0411ka1.htm).

Page 155: *We can take every growth idea and multiply its effectiveness* . . . General Electric 2003 Annual Report, "Growing in an Uncertain World," page 7.

Page 156: *Many aspiring leaders do not have the luxury* . . . Blythe McGarvie, "Going Native" *CFO Europe*, March 2003, page 49.

Page 157: *David Thomas and Keer Inkson, management professors* . . . . David C. Thomas and Kerr Inkson, *Cultural Intelligence* (Berrett-Koehler, 2004), page 20.

Page 157: *As Americans, we appear to have a natural disadvantage* . . . *Conversely, Moore finds that global managers* . . . Both quotes appear in Karl Moore, "Great Global Managers" *Across the Board*, May/June 2003. Both quotes appear in Karl Moore, "Great Global Managers" *Across the Board*, May/June 2003.

Page 158: *A global citizen attempts to eliminate national parochialism* . . . A quote from Danielle Tullier, "Jet-Setter" *Kellogg World*, June 2002, page 50.

Page 158: *The development of global citizenship also requires* . . . Kathryn Kranhold, et al., "Lost in Translation," *Wall Street Journal*, May 18, 2004.

Page 159: *Cultural differences can also affect how you approach* . . . Kevin Rubens, "Ambassadors of the Air," *HR Innovator*, May 2004, pages 31–32.

Page 161: *Bruno Angelici, executive VP,* . . . Author interviews and e-mail with Bruno Angelici.

Page 162: *McKinnell says that his exposure to other cultures offered* . . . Both quotes are from Justin Martin, "The Global CEO," *Chief Executive*, January/February 2004, pages 24–31.

Page 163: *In the past, the relationship between international* . . . Lowell L. Bryan and Jane N. Fraser, "Getting to Global," *The McKinsey Quarterly*, 1999, Number 4.

Page 165: A*s the degree of economic globalization increases* . . . Bryan and Fraser.

Pages 165–166: *At the same time, Wal-Mart is expanding into the Chinese marketplace* . . . Sarah Schafer, "A Welcome to Wal-Mart" *Newsweek International*, December 20, 2004; Jiang Jingjing, "Wal-Mart's China inventory to hit US$18 billion" *China Business Weekly*, December 2, 2004; Charles Fishman, "The Wal-Mart You Don't Know" *Fast Company*, December 2003.

Page 166: *Smart companies further realize that purchasing* . . . Lawrence M. Fisher, "Yves Doz: The Thought Leader Interview," *strategy + business*, issue 29, page 117.

Page 166: *Microsoft Corporation searches the globe* . . . Quoted in Chris Buckley, "Let a Thousand Ideas Flower," *New York Times*, September 13, 2004.

Page 166: *In December 2004, Microsoft announced* . . . Quoted in Brier Dudley, "Microsoft opening a research lab in India," *Seattle Times*, December 1, 2004.

Page 167: *In 2003, in the seventh annual* . . . *"The value is clear," says Tom Neff* . . . Quoted in Martin, page 26.

Page 167: *In 2003, in the seventh annual.* . . *"probably number four or five .* . . Quoted in Alix Nyberg, "Finance Execs Need Overseas Experience, Say CEOs," *CFO.com*, September 28, 2001.

Page 168: *Cross-cultural training is supplemental* . . . Pam George, "Lipp Service," *HR Innovator*, March 2004, page 34.

Pages 168–169: *Ready for Economic Globalization?* . . . The complete report of The National Geographic-Roper 2002 Global Geographic Literacy Survey is available at www.nationalgeographic.com/geosurvey.

Epilogue

Pages 174–175: *The first issue in timing.* . . . *When Lou Gerstner* . . . Louis V. Gerstner, *Who Says Elephants Can't Dance* (Harper Business, 2002), pages 21–22.

Pages 174–175: *The first issue in timing. . . . Southwest Airlines purposely . . .* Quoted in Kevin and Jackie Freiberg, *Nuts!* (Broadway Books, 1998), page 65.

Page 178: *"That depends a great deal on . . .* Lewis Carroll, *Alice's Adventures in Wonderland* (Dover, 1993), page 41.

Pages 178–179: *Actor Jim Carrey likes to tell this . . .* Quoted in Belinda Luscombe, "Tears of a Clown" *Time*, March 27, 1995, page 79.

Page 179: *There are two lessons . . . "Make no little plans . . .* See *Bartlett's Familiar Quotations*: Sixteenth Edition (Little Brown, 1992).

Page 179: *Once you know where you want to go . . .* Author interviews and fax from John H. Dasburg, CEO and chairman, ASTAR Air Cargo; see also Horatio Alger Association, *2001 Award Winners*, page 27.

Page 180: *This would be the professional challenge . . .* Arthur C. Martinez, *The Hard Road to the Softer Side* (Crown Business, 2000), page 78.

Pages 180–181: *So, how should you navigate the intersections . . .* Julie Daum and Carolyn Eadie, "Boards reconsidered," *Point of View*, 2003, page 25.

Page 181: *The turning point in Lou Gertsner's decision . . .* Gerstner, pages 13–17.

Page 181: *Will I learn something from this? . . .* Author interview with Susan Kronick, vice-chair, Federated Department Stores.

Page 182–183: *What Is the Leadership Learning Quotient? . . .* Stephen J. Drotter and Ram Charan, "Building Leaders at Every Level of the Leadership Pipeline," *Ivey Business Journal*, May/June 2001; see also Ram Charan, Stephen Drotter, and James Noel, *The Leadership Pipeline* (Jossey-Bass, 2000).

ACKNOWLEDGMENTS

This book could not have been written ten years ago. It required an odyssey that I never would have imagined prior to my living it. Life seemed a somewhat straight forward and directed progression as I attempted to satisfy my curiosity in different companies, ideas, people and events. Then in 1994, recognizing that if we wanted to fulfill both of our personal and career dreams, my husband and I needed to begin a journey and leave the comfort and complacency we enjoyed together in Chicago with our friends and our routines. After some emotional and intellectual angst, we embarked on an unpredictable journey, that produced the most fun and rewarding times of our professional lives.

Along the way, so many different individuals shared their friendship and knowledge with us as we moved to Maine, Indiana, New York, France and Virginia. At times, my ten years without a permanent residence reminded me of Homer's tale the vicissitudes of Odysseus' travels as he was trying to return home from the Trojan War. Yet, I would not trade the experiences, lessons, and friendships developed over the last ten years for the security a less peripatetic life might have produced. It's humbling for me to reflect on how many colleagues, mentors and friends supported my experience, providing me opportunities and responsibilities many of which exceeded my expectations.

One person who believed in me when I had many doubts was my husband, Mark. Although I have not been the most constant person—being distracted by my work, other people, or the need to keep traveling—he has stood faithfully and consistently by my side. After 22 years of marriage, I still believe the best decision I ever made was to marry Mark. His continued support during the research, writing and editing of this book is the ultimate success for me.

Today, with the completion of *Fit In, Stand Out, Mastering the FISO Factor for Success in Business and Life*, I feel as if I have come home and primary acknowledgement to those who have believed in me and helped shape this manuscript is due special friends: to Reid Boates, Mary Glenn, Ted Kinni, Dr. Brian Jaski, Lisa Halvorson and Cathy Cranston. The stories and messages I recount in this book could never have been possible if many others, about whom you will read, had not generously given their time and perspectives. Thank you to Keith Alm, Bruno Angelici, Steve Ballmer, Warren Bennis, Thierry Benoit, Bruno Bich, John Cahill, John Carl, Ram Charan, Bob Chuck, Jim Collins, Doug Conant, Kevin Cox, John Dasburg, Tom Davenport, Peter Drucker, Danny Ertel, Joe Forehand, Cathy Higgins, Rod Kramer, Susan Kronick, Pamela Forbes Leiberman, Bob Lipp, Dick Lochridge, Claudine Malone, Bernard Mohr, Philippe Rollier, Mohan Sawhney, Howard Schultz, Jeffrey Sonnefeld, Robert Thomas, Jane Magruder Watkins, Jack Welch, Dick Wood, and Meg Weston.

INDEX

INDEX

Access, 44, 107
Action
  Moulton's three domains of, 74–75
  soundness of, 76–77
  timeliness of, 69
Adaptation, 119–121
Agility, 49, 169–170
AI. *See* Appreciative inquiry
Alchemy, 33–34
Alger, Horatio, 1
Alice's Adventures in Wonderland (Carroll),
  17–18, 178
Alignment, 60
Allen, Robert, 14–15
Alliance, 89
Alm, Keith, 120–121
Ambition, 4, 5
American Journal of Sociology, 99
Angelici, Bruno, 161, 197
Apple Computer, 8
  innovation prowess of, 9

Appreciative inquiry (AI), 149–150
Archimedes of Syracuse, 89, 94, 191–192
Armstrong, Michael, 15, 129
Arthur Andersen & Company, 83–84
AT&T Corporation, 56–57, 186
Attention, 68

Bacon, Francis, 115
Baker, Wayne, 90, 105, 192
Balance, 30
Balanced judgment, 47, 150–151
Ballmer, Steve, 64, 128, 182
Bassi, Laurie, 126
Bean-counting, 37
Behavior Sciences Research Press, 25–26
Belonging, children and, 30
Belyaev, Anna, 100–101
Benefit, mutual, 100
Bennis, Warren, 75, 190
Benoit, Thierry, 90–91
Berner, Mary, 127

BIC pens. *See* SociÈtÈ BIC
Bich, Bruno, 48–49
Bich, Marcel, 48–49.188
Bollenbach, Steve, 37–38, 39
Bossidy, Larry, 38, 68–69, 146, 187
Bourgart, Joseph, 80–81
Boys and Girls Club of Chicago (BGCC), 30
Buffet, Warren, 16, 76, 190–191
Burnham, Daniel Hudson, 179
Burt, Ronald, 94, 96–97, 103–104, 192
Business
    customer-centric, 145–146
    foreign countries, values, and, 136–137
    language of, 36, 53
    mean, 28
    perspective needed by, 145
    savvy, 38
    self-selection out of, 3–4
    strategies of, 13
    system, imperatives of, 11–16
Business Week, 147

Cahill, John, 132–133
Candidates, 23–24
Career lens, financial knowledge filtered
    through, 60
Career success, 9, 20
Carl, John, 86–87, 98
Carnegie-Mellon University, 147
Carrey, Jim, 178–179, 199
Carroll, Lewis, 17
Case Western Reserve University's
    Weatherhead School of Management, 149
Catalysts. *See* FISO Factor; Global citizenship
Catalytic spectrum, 56, 87, 111, 134, 155
Center for Creative Leadership, 113
Center for Public Leadership, 22
Center for Research in Technology and
    Innovation, 146
CEOs, backgrounds of, 34
CFO Europe, 156
CFO Magazine, 140
Challenge, 149
Change
    leaders and, 121, 122
    learning requiring, 123
    necessity of, 183
    six perspectives on, 144–145
Charan, Ram, 38, 146, 187, 199

Chief Executive, 167
Children, 30–31
China
    Microsoft Corporation and, 166
    U.S. exports to, 154
    Wal-Mart and, 165–166
Choosing, juggling v., 30
Chuck, Robert, 141–142
Citizenship. *See* Global citizenship
C-level, 1, 10
    females and, 148
    FISO Factor and, 29
    hiring trends at, 167
    leaders, 112
    six agents leading to, 50
CNN/USA Today/Gallup Poll, 73–74
COGS. *See* Cost of goods sold
Collins, Jim, 44, 188
Compensation
    controversy over, 3
    executive, 3
    leaders and, 180
Competence, 25
    children and, 30–31
Competitive advantage, 165
Completeness, 78–79
Compliance, legal, 74–79
Conference Board survey, 2
    ten attributes in, 6
Confidence
    financial acuity yielding, 39, 68–69
    knowledge creating, 68
Conformity, 25
Connections, 120–121
    finding of, 64
Consensus, perspective and, 143–144
Conspiracy of silence, 122
Cooperrider, David, 149
Corporate America, 3, 40
Corporate code, 55–64
    Lieberman's cracking of, 55
    of silence, 85
Corporate consciousness, 44
Corporate culture, 174–176
Corporate personality matrix, 175–176
Corporation for Positive Change, 149
Cost of goods sold (COGS), 60
Courage, 26
Creativity, 93–95

Credibility, 24–25
Customization, 12
Cycles, economic, 1

Dasburg, John, 179–180, 199
Daschle, Tom, 85
Data generation, 66
Davenport, Tom, 42
Days sales outstanding (DSO), 58
DDI. *See* Developmental Dimensions
    International
de Geus, Arie, 126
de Leon, Ponce, 109, 193
Delphic oracle, 134
Demand flow manufacturing (DFM), 129
Deming, W. Edwards, 10
Depth, 97
Developmental Dimensions International
    (DDI), 2–3
DFM. *See* Demand flow manufacturing
Differences, cultural, 159, 160
Disciplined thought, 44
Disney, Roy E., 42–43
Disney, Roy O., 42–43
Dissent, 85
Diversity, 147
Dodson, Charles Lutwidge. *See* Carroll,
    Lewis
Drotter, Stephen, 182, 199
Drucker, Peter, 110–111, 194
DSO. *See* Days sales outstanding
Dudley, George, 25–26, 187

The Economist, 160
Economy. *See* Global economy
Eisner, Michael, 42–43
Emigrant, immigrant v., 47–48
Empathy, 137–139
Employees
    education for, 85
    ideas of, 61
    strategies needed by, 68
    successful, 11, 163
Employers, helpfulness of, 5
Enron, 39
Ertel, Danny, 106
Entrepreneurial fiefdoms, 163
Ethics, 74–76, 75
Ethos, 75, 76

Eureka moments, 94, 95
Executive search industry, 2

Failure, 124–125
Farrington, Hugh, 140
Fast Company, 9, 165
Favors, 100–101
Females, C-level and, 148
The Fifth Discipline (Senge), 10, 126
Financial acuity, 36–39
    ABCs of, 69–70
    "bean-counting" and, 37
    catalytic spectrum for, 56, 68
    confidence yielded by, 39, 68–69
    dearth of, 56
    fostering of, 66–68
    integrity's tempering of, 39
    leaders and, 55
    organizational success and, 67
Findings, acting on, 65–66
Fiorina, Carly, 141
FISO Factor, 29–31
    catalysts, 35–51, 178
    C-level and, 29
    elements of, 30–31
    fitting-in and, 29
    leaders and, 33, 50
    standing-out and, 29
    timing, 174–178
    trust's supporting of, 86
Fitting-in
    building trust and, 20–21
    considerations for, 177–178
    credibility and, 24–25
    FISO Factor and, 29
    getting in v., 22
    global citizenship and, 170
    integration and, 19, 20
    linkages and, 90
    process of, 20
    standing-out and, 27–28
Five whys technique, 115
5As of learning, 121–125
    financial focus process, 122
    website for, 123
Fluency, financial, 58
Followers, 23
Forehand, Joe, 138–139, 196
Fountain of Youth, 109

France, financial community of, 159
Frappucino, 119–120
Frustration, 18

Garvin, David, 118
Gender
    diversity, 147
    perspective and, 148
General Electric Company, 45, 146, 154, 197
Gerstner, Lou, 174–175, 181, 199
Getting in, fitting in v., 22
Gilmartin, Raymond, 40–41
Giving, getting v., 100–101
Global citizenship, 47–49
    ABCs of, 170
    agility yielded by, 49, 169–170
    capturing power of, 164
    catalysts of, 159–160, 169
    catalytic spectrum for, 155
    development of, 158–159
    fitting-in with, 170
    international cooperation and, 162
    learning opportunities created by, 169
    open approach of, 160
    SociÈtÈ BIC and, 48
    standing-out with, 170–171
Global corporation, 12
Global economy
    changes created by, 156
    ramifications of, 154
Global journey, 159–160
Global knowledge, 166–167
Global leadership, 156–164
Global management, 156, 157–158, 167–168
Global organization, 165–168
Global stimulation, 162–164
Globalization, 154
    increasing economic, 165
    opportunities offered by, 166
    readiness for, 168–169, 198
Glova, Judi, 95–96
Goals
    accomplishing, 9
    aligning of, 61
    pursuing common, 163
    setting, 179
    work, 18
Golden Rule, 79
Granovetter, Mark, 99–100

Great Crash, 110
Groupthink, 103

Han Dynasty, 14
Hannaford Bros. Co., 2, 27, 66, 98
    learning groups at, 127–128
Harvard Business Review, 28, 188
Harvard Business School, 118, 190
Harvard's Kennedy School of Government, 22, 28
Heifitz, Ronald, 22–23, 186
Helmsley, Leona, 134–135
Hewlett-Packard Company, 141
Higgins, Cathy, 115
Honeywell International, 38

I Ching (Book of Changes), 13
Iansiti, Marco, 106–107
IBM, 174
Immelt, Jeffrey, 146, 154–155
Immigrant, emigrant v., 47–48
In Search of Excellence (Peters), 104–105
Inclusivity, 146
    leaders and, 148
Information, staunching flow of, 116
Innovation, 13
    learning yielding, 45, 128–129
Insight, 137
Integration, 11
    business systems and, 16
    fitting-in process of, 19, 20
    reengineering and, 13–14
Integrity, 39–41
    ABCs of, 88
    actions measured by, 41
    bar of, 82
    catalytic spectrum for, 87
    demands of, 80–82
    ethos and, 75
    financial acuity tempered by, 39
    fluctuations of, 82
    leadership with/without, 39, 72, 78
    myths of, 84–85
    North Star and, 71
    nuances of, 74
    organizational, 83–86
    public's view of, 40
    silence and, 86
    standing-out and, 80

Integrity *(continued)*
　　three facets of, 75
　　transparency and, 78
　　trust yielded by, 41
Intelligence, cultural, 157
Internal Revenue Service, 143–144
International assignments, 167–168
Internet
　　craze, 16
　　gold, 15–16, 186
Isdell, Neville, 142

Jobs, Steve, 8–9, 43, 186
Johnson & Johnson, 46–47
Juggling, choosing v., 30

Kahl, Jack, 67
Kampouris, Emanuel, 129
Keiretsu system, 157
Kelley, Robert, 147
Kelley, Tom, 15, 186
Kellogg Graduate School of Management,
　　98–99, 125, 161
Kellogg Innovation Network, 125
Kennedy, John F., 115
The Keystone Advantage (Iansiti, Levien), 106
King, Martin Luther, Jr., 136
Kleiner, Art, 95
Knowledge
　　acting on, 65
　　adapting of, 119–121
　　adoption of, 112–118
　　confidence created by, 68
　　financial, 59, 60
　　generating, 127
　　global, 166–167
　　leaders seeking of, 113
Korn Ferry recruiting firm, 167
Kouzes, Jim, 24
KPMG survey, 73
Kraemer, Harry, 138
Kraft Foods, 69
Kramer, Roderick, 120, 194
Kreuger, Ivar, 72–73
Kroc, Ray, 114
Kronick, Susan, 181–182, 199

Language
　　business, 36, 53

Language *(continued)*
　　of finance, 59
　　understanding basics of, 59
"Law and Manners" (Moulton), 74–75
Leader(s)
　　challenge for, 149
　　as change agents, 121, 122
　　C-level, 112
　　compensation and, 180
　　dissent and, 85
　　eliciting support by, 143
　　employee ideas and, 61
　　equipping current/future, 18
　　fatal flaws of, 113
　　financial acuity of, 55
　　finding of, 2
　　FISO Factor and, 33
　　as frontline generals, 122–123
　　global managers as, 156, 157–158
　　holistic management by, 79
　　immigrant mindset and, 48
　　inclusivity and, 148
　　inner, 111
　　insight mastered by, 137
　　integrity of, 72
　　judging, 83
　　knowledge sought by, 113
　　lever of alliance and, 89
　　options evaluated by, 179–180
　　perspectives and, 133–136
　　points of view sought by, 46
　　questions asked by, 44–45
　　rules maintained by, 41
　　soundness in, 76
　　standing-out by, 27
　　system thinking of, 9–11
　　transformation by, 111
　　translating/transferring expertise by,
　　　164
　　travel required by, 163
　　unsoundness of, 78
Leadership. *See also* Global leadership
　　ABCs of, 7
　　alchemy and, 34
　　aspirations to, 5, 11
　　Conference Board survey on, 2, 6
　　decisions of, 131
　　effectiveness, 19, 97
　　ethics and, 75

Leadership *(continued)*
  FISO Factors needed for, 50
  hierarchy, 23
  integrity and, 39, 78
  international experience and, 161, 162
  journey of, 184
  learning quotient, 182–183
  opportunities for, 1, 2
  platform, 49–51
  positions, 1
  scarcity, 2
  shortage of, 5
  study of, 34
  success, 7, 10, 19
  visibility required by, 26
The Leadership Pipeline (Charan, Drotter, Noel), 182–183, 199
Learning, 44–45
  5As of, 121–125
  ABCs of, 130
  capitalizing on, 160
  catalytic spectrum for, 111
  change and, 123
  corporate consciousness and, 44
  creating an organization for, 126–128
  four skills of, 118–119
  global citizenship and, 169
  innovation yielded by, 45, 128–129
  lifelong, 119
  organizational, 126, 127
  perfection and, 123
  quotient, 182–183
  refining, 123
  Sawhney on, 125–126
  self-directed, 110
  spreading of, 127
Levien, Roy, 106–107
Lieberman, Pamela Forbes, 53–55, 60, 189
  financial acuity displayed by, 55–56
LIF Group, process model of, 122
Lincoln, Abraham, 143
Linkages, 42–44
  ABCs of, 108
  academic affiliation, 98
  access yielded by, 44, 107
  breadth/depth of, 97
  catalytic agent of, 95, 103
  community, 99
  competitive advantages of, 92–96

Linkages *(continued)*
  creating/maintaining, 96–102, 177
  creativity and, 94
  depth and, 97
  external, 96
  fitting-in and, 90
  investing in, 101
  networks and, 89
  opportunity created via, 92–93
  performance and, 42
  preexisting, 98
  productivity and, 96
  SociÈtÈ BIC and, 91
  standing-out and, 90
  tapping group, 105
  "touch-tone approach" to, 101–103
  valuing, 105–106
  viral marketing and, 104–105
  work related, 98
Lipp, Bob, 68
Listening, 116–118
  active, 117–118
  effective, 118
  non-emotional, 117
  perspectives and, 144
Literacy, financial, 67
Lochridge, Dick, 102–103

Maccoby, Michael, 27–28, 46–47, 187, 188
Macy, William H., 135, 196
Malone, Claudine, 148–149
Management. *See* Global management
Manco, Inc., 67–68
Market pressure, 7
Marketing, one-to-one, 12
Marriot Corporation, 37
  identity of, 38
Marriot, J.W., Jr., 37, 187
Martin, Dick, 129, 189, 195
Martinez, Arthur, 180
Matrix
  corporate personality, 175–176
  skills/values, 23–24
Maxwell, John, 26
McKinnell, Henry, 162
McKinsey and Company, 163, 165
McVicker, Bob, 117
Merck & Company, Inc., 40–41
Metanationals, 48

Microsoft Corporation, 64, 82–83, 198
 China and, 166
Millken, Michael, 40
Mindset, limitations of, 61–62
Misconduct, 73
Mistakes, cost of, 125
Mohr, Bernard, 150
Moore, Karl, 157–158, 197
Moulton, John Fletcher, 74–75, 190
Multitasking, 146

Nathan, Arte, 127
National Geographic-Roper 2002 Global
 Geographic Literacy Survey, 168–169,
 198
Nationality, transcending of, 156–159
Neff, Tom, 167, 196
Networking
 social, 104
 tactics, 101
Networks
 central connections to, 106–107
 danger of closed, 103
 linkages and, 89
New Economy, 34–35
Newton, Isaac, 131, 195
Noel, James, 182, 199
North Star, 189–190
 integrity and, 71
 spiritual/mythical significance of, 72
Numbers, digging into, 64–65

Objectives, SociÈtÈ BIC's, 62–63
Opportunity
 leadership, 1, 2
 linkages and, 92–93
Organization. *See* Global organization
Organizational integrity, 83–84
Organizational learning, 126, 127
Organizational perspective
 creation of, 145–149
 diversity and, 147
Organizational success
 code of, 10
 creating, 164
 financial acuity and, 67
Outsourcing, 64

ParaComm Partners, 144

Parmalat Corporation, 8
PDAs, 96
Pepsi Bottling Group (PBG), 101, 132–133,
 192–193
Perceptions, 139–140
Perfection
 learning and, 123
 progress and, 123–124
Performance
 corporate goals aligned to, 61
 linkages and, 42
 organizational, 124
 past, 124
Perspective(s), 46–47. *See also* Organizational
 perspective
 ABCs of, 151–152
 applications of, 145
 balanced judgment yielded by, 47, 150–151
 broadness of, 136
 business's need of, 145
 catalytic spectrum for, 134
 consensus and, 143–144
 customer's, 146
 diversity and, 46
 empathy and, 137–139
 encouraging individual, 146
 external, 132–133
 informed, shared, 133, 140
 internal, 132
 leaders and, 133–136
 listening and, 144
 loss of, 135
 magnet, 140–142
 organizational, 145–149
 other people's, 137–145
 stakeholder's, 141
Peters, Tom, 104–105
Pfizer, Inc., 162
Pixar Animation Studios, 43
Point of view, 46
Position, changing of, 5
Posner, Barry, 24, 187
Precepts, often forgotten, 7–9
Productive narcissists, 28
Productivity, 95–96
 external linkages and, 96
 increasing, 4
 Welch's explanation of, 45
Progress, perfection and, 123–124

Questions, 115–116

Rashid, Richard, 166
Reflection, 119–120
Relationships, 97
    international business/corporate head-
        quarters, 163
    sharing and, 100
Reluctance, psychology of, 25–26
Responsibility, 84
Return on relationships (ROR), 106
Robber Barons, 40
Rockefeller, John D., 4, 5, 185
Rollier, Philippe, 180
ROR. *See* Return on relationships
Rossotti, Charles, 143–144, 196
Russell Reynolds Associates, 139

Sara Lee Corporation, 60–61, 93, 120–121,
    161
Sarbanes-Oxley Act, 39, 66, 81
    provisions of, 85
Sattelberger, Thomas, 159
Sawhney, Mohanbir, 146, 195
Scandals, financial, 7
Schultz, Howard, 114, 119–120, 194
Scientific Revolution, 33
Selman, Jim, 144–145, 196
Senge, Peter, 10, 126, 195
Shareholder value, 11
Sharing, relationships and, 100
Silence, 85, 86, 122
Skilling, Jeffery, 39
Social networking, 104
Société BIC, 48–49
    financial fluency lacking in, 58
    global citizenship and, 48
    linkages and, 91
    objectives at, 62–63
Society for Human Resource
        Management/*Fortune* survey, 148
Sonnenfeld, Jeffrey, 82
Soundness, 76–78
Spencer Stuart recruiting firm, 167
Srivastva, Suresh, 149
St. Ignatius's Test, 81–82, 191
St. Paul Travelers, 68
Stakeholders, perspective of, 141
Standard Oil Company, 4

Standing-out
    career success and, 20
    example of, 27
    FISO Factor and, 29
    fitting-in and, 27–28
    focusing on, 177
    global citizenship and, 170–171
    integrity and, 80
    leaders and, 27
    linkages and, 90
    transformation and, 19, 20
Stanford University, 120
Starbucks Coffee Company, 114, 119–120
Strategies, identifying of, 59–60
Success. *See also* Organizational success
    basis for career, 9
    employee, 11, 163
    final word on, 184
    leadership/organizational, 7, 10, 19
    standing-out and, 20
Sull, Donald, 75–76, 190
Support, leader's eliciting of, 143
Systems, 11–16
    information, 11
    performance boundaries and, 10
    requirements of successful, 16
    thinking, 10–11

Tanzi, Calisto, 8
Technology, 156
Thinking for a Living (Maxwell), 26
Thomas, Robert, 75, 190
3i Group, 105–106
Thull, Jeff, 115
Timing, 174–178
Touch-tone approach, 101–103
Toyota, 116
    five whys technique of, 115
Training, 5
    cross-cultural, 168
Transformation, 11
    breakthroughs, 15
    business systems and, 16
    differentiation, change, and, 12
    FISO Factor catalysts of, 178
    leaders and, 111
    standing-out process of, 19, 20
Transparency, 78
Trosten-Bloom, Amanda, 149

TruServ Corporation, 54, 60
Trust, 20–21
   Corporate America's creation of, 40
   crisis of, 73
   FISO Factor supported by, 86
   integrity's yielding of, 41

University of Chicago, 21, 22

Values, 175–176
Viewpoints, 142
Viral marketing, 104–105
Visibility, 26
Vital Signs, Inc., 80–81

The Wall Street Journal, 95–96, 155
Wal-Mart Stores, Inc., 83, 198
   China and, 165–166
Walt Disney Company, 38
   Eisner's creation of linkages at, 42–43

Walter, John, 56–57
Walton, Sam, 165
Waterman, Bob, 104–105
Watkins, Jane Magruder, 150
Welch, Jack, 26–27
   productivity explained by, 45
   retirement of, 146
Weston, Meg, 99, 192
What is, what could be v., 128–129
Whitney, Ruth, 29
Wilson, John, 167
Wood, Richard D., Jr., 78–79
Work, framing of, 61–62, 63
World, learning from, 160

Yin and yang, 12–13

Zen Buddhists, 117

ABOUT THE AUTHOR

Blythe McGarvie, a dynamic keynote speaker and author of numerous articles on business leadership and strategy, has more than two decades of experience designing and implementing major corporate financial initiatives. Ms. McGarvie is an entertaining, effective presenter who enables individuals and companies to "Release the Leader Within" and to profit from "The FISO Factor." She is the founder and president of Leadership for International Finance, a team of successful consultants drawn from the ranks of senior-level executives in various functional and industry specialties, who provides strategic and financial advice to help clients achieve their corporate objectives (www.LIFgroup.com).

Ms. McGarvie draws on a vast experience base, including service on the boards of directors of Accenture Ltd., Pepsi Bottling Group, St. Paul Travelers, Lafarge North America, and Wawa Inc. She further draws on her past work experience as chief financial officer for BIC Group, based in Paris, and as executive vice president and chief financial officer of Hannaford Bros. Co., a Fortune 500 food retailer. She also has held senior financial positions at Sara Lee Corporation and Kraft Foods. Ms. McGarvie is a Certified Public Accountant and holds an M.B.A. from the Kellogg School of Management. Recently, she was appointed Senior Fellow at Kellogg Innovation Network of the Kellogg School of Management.

This broad experience gives Ms. McGarvie the ability to unlock potential in companies and individuals. Audiences, from line managers to CEOs, benefit from Ms. McGarvie's insights on how to get things done. She is available for speaking engagements or consulting and would be delighted to work with you or your company. She can be contacted at: bmcgarvie@LIFgroup.com.